Dream Costa Rica: A Travel Preparation Guide.

D1519814

Daniel Hunter

TABLE OF CONTENTS

Chapter 1. Introduction to Costa Rica

1.1 Overview of Costa Rica

Costa Rica, often referred to as the "Rich Coast," is a captivating Central American gem renowned for its unparalleled natural beauty, diverse ecosystems, and warm hospitality. Nestled between Nicaragua to the north and Panama to the south, this small but remarkable country packs an extraordinary punch for travelers of all kinds. Costa Rica's striking geography encompasses tropical rainforests, pristine beaches, majestic volcanoes, and lush cloud forests, making it a playground for nature enthusiasts and adventure seekers.

The country is a biodiversity hotspot, hosting an astonishing array of wildlife, including howler monkeys, colorful parrots, and elusive jaguars. In fact, a quarter of its land is preserved within national parks and reserves, offering visitors an opportunity to explore thriving ecosystems and witness the wonders of the natural world.

Beyond its natural wonders, Costa Rica also embraces a "Pura Vida" way of life, which translates to "pure life." It's a philosophy that emphasizes a laid-back and stress-free existence, promoting happiness and well-being. Travelers can expect warm and friendly encounters with the locals, who are often eager to share their culture and traditions.

Costa Rica's attractions cater to a wide spectrum of interests. Adventure seekers can indulge in thrilling activities such as zip-lining through the treetops, white-water rafting, or surfing on the Pacific and Caribbean coasts. For those in search of relaxation and wellness, the country offers rejuvenating spa retreats, natural hot springs, and yoga centers in tranquil settings.

Food lovers will delight in the country's culinary offerings, with an emphasis on fresh and local ingredients. Traditional Costa Rican cuisine boasts mouthwatering dishes like gallo pinto (rice and beans), casado (a typical meal with rice, beans, and a choice of protein), and a variety of tropical fruits and seafood.

Whether you're a solo traveler, a family with children, or a couple looking for a romantic getaway, Costa Rica welcomes all with open arms. It's a destination that invites you to explore, connect with nature, and immerse yourself in a way of life that celebrates the simple joys. Costa Rica is a place where you can truly experience the essence of "Pura Vida."

1.2 Why Visit Costa Rica?

Costa Rica, often referred to as the "Rich Coast," is a tropical paradise that beckons travelers from all corners of the globe. There are countless reasons why this small but vibrant country in Central America is a must-visit destination. Whether you're a solo traveler seeking adventure, a family looking for a memorable vacation, or a couple in search of romance, Costa Rica has something to offer everyone. Here are some compelling reasons why you should consider making Costa Rica your next travel destination.

1. Breathtaking Natural Beauty: Costa Rica is renowned for its stunning landscapes, from pristine beaches along the Pacific and Caribbean coasts to lush rainforests, towering volcanoes, and serene cloud forests. The country's diverse geography provides endless opportunities for exploration and adventure.

2. Incredible Biodiversity: Despite its small size, Costa Rica boasts an astounding variety of wildlife and plant species. It's home to many national parks and reserves, making it a paradise for nature lovers, birdwatchers, and wildlife enthusiasts. You might spot howler monkeys, colorful toucans, or even elusive jaguars during your visit.

3. Eco-Tourism Haven: If you're passionate about responsible travel and eco-tourism, Costa Rica sets the gold standard. The country is committed to sustainability, and you'll find numerous eco-lodges, wildlife conservation efforts, and sustainable tour operators. It's an ideal destination for those who want to explore nature while leaving a minimal ecological footprint.

4. Adventure Awaits: For adrenaline junkies, Costa Rica offers a treasure trove of adventure activities. Try zip-lining through the rainforest canopy, white-water rafting on exhilarating rivers, surfing on world-class waves, or hiking to the summit of an active volcano. The options are endless.

5. Welcoming Culture: Costa Ricans, known as "Ticos" and "Ticas," are famous for their warmth and friendliness. You'll find the locals to be welcoming and ready to share their culture and traditions with you. Embrace the "Pura Vida" lifestyle, which means living life to the fullest and enjoying every moment.

6. Varied Experiences: Costa Rica isn't a one-size-fits-all destination. It offers a diverse range of experiences, from romantic getaways for couples to educational opportunities for families and solo adventures for the intrepid traveler. There's something for everyone here.

7. Delicious Cuisine: Foodies will be delighted by Costa Rican cuisine. Sample traditional dishes like "gallo pinto" (rice and beans), fresh seafood, and tropical fruits. Don't forget to savor a cup of locally grown coffee, which is some of the finest in the world.

8. Safe and Stable: Costa Rica is known for its political stability and safety, making it an ideal destination for travelers of all kinds. It's one of the safest countries in Central America, which adds to the peace of mind during your stay.

In summary, Costa Rica offers a diverse and captivating travel experience that extends well beyond its stunning landscapes. Whether you seek adventure, natural wonders, cultural immersion, or relaxation on pristine beaches, Costa Rica has it all. The country's commitment to sustainability and preservation of its natural beauty makes it a destination that not only leaves a lasting impression but also a positive impact on the planet. So, pack your bags and get ready to experience the pura vida in this enchanting Central American gem.

1.3 When to Visit

Costa Rica is a year-round destination, but the timing of your visit can greatly influence your experience. The country's diverse climate and natural beauty make it an appealing destination at any time of the year. Here's a breakdown of the different seasons and what to expect during each:

1. Dry Season (December to April):

- The dry season is the most popular time to visit Costa Rica. The weather is consistently sunny and dry.
- Ideal for beach lovers, hikers, and wildlife enthusiasts.
- Many festivals and cultural events take place during this period.

2. Green Season (May to November):
- Also known as the "green season" or "rainy season," this period experiences occasional rain showers.
- The landscape is lush and vibrant, making it a fantastic time for photographers and nature lovers.
- Fewer tourists, meaning less crowded attractions and lower prices.

3. Rainy Season (September to November):
- This period can bring heavier and more consistent rainfall, particularly on the Pacific coast.
- It's a great time for surfers, as the waves are more consistent.
- The lush rainforest is at its most vibrant during this season.

4. Shoulder Season (May, June, and November):
- This transitional period offers a balance between lower prices and fewer tourists.

- You may experience occasional showers, but the weather can be pleasant.

Ultimately, the best time to visit Costa Rica depends on your interests and priorities. If you prefer sunny, dry weather, the dry season is ideal. However, if you want to explore lush rainforests, experience fewer crowds, and enjoy budget-friendly options, the green season might be your choice. Be sure to consider your travel preferences and activities when planning your Costa Rican adventure.

Chapter 2. Getting Ready for Your Trip

2.1 Passport and Visa Information

When planning your trip to Costa Rica, one of the first essential considerations is your passport and visa requirements. Here is a detailed overview of the passport and visa information you need to know before traveling to this beautiful Central American country.

Passport Requirements:

- To enter Costa Rica, your passport must be valid for at least six months beyond your planned departure date from the country.
- Ensure that your passport has at least one blank page for entry and exit stamps.

Visa Requirements:
- Citizens of many countries, including the United States, Canada, and most European nations, do not require a visa for stays of up to 90 days in Costa Rica for tourism, business, or family visits. Check the official website of the Costa Rican embassy or consulate in your home country to verify visa requirements specific to your nationality.

Tourist Visas:
- Tourist visas are typically issued upon arrival at the airport in Costa Rica or land borders. The immigration officer will stamp your passport with the date of entry and the permitted length of stay, which is usually up to 90 days.
- For travelers planning to stay longer than 90 days or engage in activities like work, study, or volunteering, it is essential to apply for the appropriate visa before arriving in Costa Rica.

Visa Extension:

- If you wish to extend your stay beyond the initially granted period, it's possible to apply for an extension at the nearest immigration office. Extensions are usually granted in 30-day increments, and there is a fee associated with this process.

Important Notes:
- Ensure that your return or onward ticket is booked before arriving in Costa Rica. Immigration officials may ask for proof of your departure plans.
- Keep a copy of your passport, visa (if applicable), and other essential travel documents in a safe place while traveling. It's also a good idea to have digital copies stored securely.

Special Requirements:
- For some nationalities, there may be additional entry requirements or restrictions. It's crucial to check with the Costa Rican embassy or consulate in your country to confirm specific details.

By understanding the passport and visa requirements for Costa Rica, you can ensure a smooth and hassle-free entry into this captivating destination. Always double-check the latest regulations before your trip, as immigration policies can change, and it's essential to be well-prepared for your adventure in this tropical paradise.

2.2 Vaccinations and Health Precautions

When embarking on your adventure to Costa Rica, it's essential to prioritize your health and well-being. The following information will guide you on the necessary vaccinations and health precautions to ensure a safe and enjoyable trip.

1. Routine Vaccinations:

   - Ensure that you are up to date on routine vaccinations such as measles, mumps, rubella (MMR), diphtheria-tetanus-pertussis, varicella (chickenpox), and the annual flu shot.

2. Hepatitis A:

   - Consider getting a hepatitis A vaccination, as it can be contracted through contaminated food and water.

3. Hepatitis B:

   - Depending on your travel plans and activities, you may need a hepatitis B vaccine. Consult with your healthcare provider to assess your specific risk.

4. Typhoid:

   - Typhoid vaccinations are recommended for travelers who plan to explore rural areas where sanitation and food safety may be less reliable.

5. Yellow Fever:

   - Yellow fever vaccination is not required for entry to Costa Rica. However, if you are arriving from a country with a risk of yellow fever transmission, you may need to show proof of vaccination.

6. Malaria and Dengue:

   - Some areas in Costa Rica have a risk of malaria and dengue. Consult with a healthcare professional about antimalarial medications if you plan to visit these regions. To prevent dengue, use mosquito repellent and take other preventive measures.

Health Precautions:

- Water: It's advisable to drink bottled water or use a water purifier if you are unsure of the quality of the local water supply.
- Food: Enjoy the delicious Costa Rican cuisine, but exercise caution when consuming street food. Stick to reputable restaurants and ensure food is thoroughly cooked.
- Sun Protection: Costa Rica's sun can be intense. Use sunscreen, wear a hat, and protect your skin.
- Insect Protection: As mentioned, mosquitoes can be a concern in some areas. Use insect repellent and wear long-sleeved clothing in the evenings.

Travel Medical Kit:

Pack a small medical kit with essentials such as over-the-counter medications, first-aid supplies, and any prescription medications you may need.

Health Insurance:

Don't forget to obtain travel insurance that covers medical emergencies. Check the details of your policy and ensure it includes coverage for Costa Rica.

Before your trip, it's highly recommended to consult with a healthcare professional or a travel medicine specialist who can provide personalized advice based on your health history and the specific regions you plan to visit in Costa Rica. Following these precautions will help you stay healthy and enjoy your journey to the fullest.

2.3 Travel Insurance

Travel insurance is an essential component of planning your trip to Costa Rica, ensuring peace of mind and protection against unexpected circumstances. Whether you're a solo traveler, a family with kids, or a couple embarking on a romantic getaway, having the right travel insurance in place is crucial. Here's why it matters and what to consider:

Why You Need Travel Insurance:

1. Medical Emergencies: Costa Rica boasts lush rainforests, pristine beaches, and thrilling adventure activities. However, accidents can happen. Travel insurance covers medical expenses in case of injury or illness, including hospitalization, doctor visits, and even medical evacuation if necessary.

2. Trip Cancellations: Sometimes, unforeseen events like a family emergency or airline strikes can

force you to cancel your trip. Travel insurance can reimburse you for non-refundable trip costs.

3. Lost or Delayed Luggage: No one wants to arrive in paradise only to find their luggage missing or delayed. Travel insurance can provide compensation for lost, stolen, or delayed baggage.

4. Travel Delays: Delays due to weather or other unforeseen events can disrupt your itinerary. Travel insurance can cover additional expenses such as accommodation and meals.

5. Adventure Sports Coverage: If you plan to engage in adventure activities like zip-lining, surfing, or scuba diving, ensure your policy includes coverage for these activities.

Choosing the Right Travel Insurance:

1. Coverage Levels: Consider the coverage limits for medical expenses, trip cancellations, and other benefits. Make sure they align with the type of trip you're planning.

2. Pre-Existing Conditions: If you have pre-existing medical conditions, check if they are covered and if there are any exclusions.

3. Adventure Sports: If you're an adventure enthusiast, verify that the policy covers activities you plan to participate in.

4. Exclusions: Read the policy carefully to understand what is not covered, as exclusions vary among insurers.

5. Emergency Assistance: Ensure your policy offers 24/7 emergency assistance. You might need help at any time during your journey.

6. Length of Coverage: Your insurance should cover the entire duration of your stay in Costa Rica.

Where to Purchase Travel Insurance:

1. Online Providers: Numerous reputable online providers offer travel insurance tailored to your needs.

2. Credit Cards: Some credit cards offer travel insurance as a cardholder benefit. Check the coverage provided and whether it meets your requirements.

3. Travel Agencies: Your travel agency can often assist in purchasing travel insurance.

When choosing your policy, it's important to compare different options and select one that provides the best coverage for your specific needs. Keep a copy of your insurance policy and contact information with you during your travels, and consider sharing this information with a trusted person back home. With the right travel insurance, you can explore the beauty of Costa Rica with confidence, knowing that you're prepared for whatever your journey may bring.

2.4 Packing Tips

Packing for your Costa Rica adventure is an exciting part of trip preparation. This tropical paradise offers diverse landscapes, climates, and activities, so it's essential to be well-prepared. Here are some packing tips to ensure you have everything you need for your Costa Rica journey:

1. Lightweight Clothing:
   - Lightweight, breathable clothing is a must. Opt for moisture-wicking fabrics, as Costa Rica's climate can be hot and humid.

2. Swimwear:

- Don't forget your swimsuits! You'll find plenty of opportunities to enjoy Costa Rica's stunning beaches, rivers, and waterfalls.

3. Comfortable Footwear:
   - Sturdy, comfortable shoes are crucial for exploring. Bring hiking boots or sturdy sandals for outdoor adventures and a pair of casual shoes for city outings.

4. Rain Gear:
   - Pack a compact, waterproof jacket or poncho. Rain showers can occur, especially during the wet season, and you'll want to stay dry during your activities.

5. Sun Protection:
   - Sunscreen, sunglasses, and a wide-brimmed hat are essential. Costa Rica's sun can be strong, and protecting your skin and eyes is important.

6. Insect Repellent:
   - Costa Rica is home to various insects, especially in the rainforests. Bring a good quality insect repellent to keep the bugs at bay.

7. Travel Adapters:

- Ensure you have the right plug adapter for your electronic devices, as Costa Rica uses Type A and Type B electrical outlets.

8. Travel Documents:
   - Keep your passport, visa, travel insurance, and other important documents in a waterproof and secure travel pouch.

9. Medications and First Aid:
   - Pack any necessary prescription medications and a basic first-aid kit. It's also a good idea to carry over-the-counter remedies for common ailments.

10. Backpack or Day Bag:
    - A lightweight daypack is useful for carrying essentials during day trips and hikes.

11. Reusable Water Bottle:
    - Costa Rica has excellent tap water. Bring a reusable water bottle to reduce plastic waste and stay hydrated.

12. Camera and Binoculars:
    - Capture the natural beauty of Costa Rica by packing your camera and binoculars for wildlife and bird watching.

13. Money:
   - Bring some local currency (Colón) and a credit card. Most places in Costa Rica accept credit cards, but having some cash is convenient, especially in rural areas.

14. Ziplock Bags:
   - These are handy for protecting electronics and keeping items dry in case of rain.

15. Snorkeling Gear:
   - If you plan to explore the underwater world, consider bringing your snorkeling gear to save on rental fees.

16. Language Guidebook:
   - A pocket-sized Spanish phrasebook can be incredibly helpful, especially if you're venturing off the beaten path.

Remember that packing light is key. You can always do laundry or buy items locally if needed. Tailor your packing list to the specific activities and regions you plan to visit, and you'll be well-prepared for an unforgettable trip in Costa Rica.

Chapter 3. Solo Travelers

3.1 Solo Travel Tips

Traveling solo in Costa Rica can be an incredibly rewarding experience, allowing you the freedom to explore at your own pace and immerse yourself in the country's stunning natural beauty and vibrant culture. To make the most of your solo adventure, consider these tips:

1. Plan and Research: Before you depart, do your research. Understand the country's geography, weather, and the best destinations for solo travelers. Costa Rica offers a wide range of experiences, from beaches to rainforests, so plan according to your interests.

2. Safety First: While Costa Rica is generally safe for tourists, it's wise to take precautions. Keep an eye on your belongings, especially in crowded areas. Stay in well-reviewed accommodations and be aware of your surroundings, especially after dark.

3. Learn Some Spanish: While many Costa Ricans speak English, especially in tourist areas, knowing some basic Spanish phrases can go a long way. It can help you communicate with locals and make your trip more immersive.

4. Use Local Transportation: Costa Rica has an efficient public transportation system. Utilize buses and shared shuttles to get around, which not only saves money but also allows you to interact with locals and enjoy the scenic routes.

5. Connect with Other Travelers: Costa Rica is a popular destination for solo travelers, so you'll likely meet others along the way. Hostels and common travel spots are great places to strike up conversations and maybe even find travel companions.

6. Pack Light: Traveling solo means you're responsible for your luggage, so pack light and

efficiently. Opt for a backpack rather than heavy suitcases for ease of movement.

7. Join Tours and Activities: Participating in guided tours or activities can be a great way to meet people and explore the country safely. Whether it's a jungle hike, a surfing lesson, or a wildlife tour, there are plenty of options.

8. Stay Active and Adventurous: Costa Rica is a paradise for adventure seekers. Embrace the opportunities for ziplining, whitewater rafting, hiking, and more. These activities not only thrill but also introduce you to like-minded travelers.

9. Respect Nature and Environment: Costa Rica is renowned for its biodiversity and commitment to conservation. As a solo traveler, take time to appreciate the natural beauty and do your part to protect it by following eco-friendly practices.

10. Trust Your Instincts: While solo travel can be liberating, always trust your instincts. If something doesn't feel right or safe, it's okay to change your plans or seek assistance from local authorities or fellow travelers.

11. Keep Important Documents Secure: Make copies of your passport, ID, and other essential documents. Keep the originals in a secure location and have digital backups stored on a cloud service.

Remember, solo travel in Costa Rica can be a life-changing experience. Embrace the culture, nature, and adventure at your own pace, and you'll likely leave with unforgettable memories and a sense of personal growth.

3.2 Safety Considerations

Costa Rica is a beautiful and diverse country that offers a wealth of experiences for solo travelers. While it's generally considered safe for tourists, it's essential to be aware of safety considerations to ensure a worry-free journey. Here are some tips for solo travelers in Costa Rica:

1. Research Your Destinations: Before you go, research the areas you plan to visit. Some places may be more remote or less developed, so understanding the local conditions and potential risks is crucial.

2. Stay in Well-Established Areas: Opt for accommodations in well-established tourist areas. These places often have better security measures in

place, and you're more likely to meet fellow travelers.

3. Share Your Itinerary: Let someone back home or at your accommodation know your travel plans, including where you're going and when you expect to return. This can be a helpful safety net.

4. Use Reputable Transportation: When moving between destinations, use reputable transportation providers. Be cautious when accepting rides from strangers, and if you're renting a car, make sure it's from a reliable company.

5. Carry Minimal Valuables: Leave expensive jewelry, electronics, and large sums of cash at home or in a secure place. Travel with only the essentials and keep an eye on your belongings at all times.

6. Be Mindful of Your Surroundings: While Costa Rica is generally safe, it's wise to be aware of your surroundings. Avoid walking alone in unlit areas at night and be cautious in unfamiliar neighborhoods.

7. Learn Basic Spanish: While many Costa Ricans speak English, especially in tourist areas, learning some basic Spanish can be extremely helpful in communication and emergencies.

8. Use ATMs with Caution: Use ATMs during daylight hours and in secure locations. Be discreet when withdrawing money, and check the machine for any suspicious devices.

9. Stay Informed: Keep updated on local news and any travel advisories for Costa Rica. Your embassy or consulate can provide useful information and assistance in case of emergencies.

10. Trust Your Instincts: If something doesn't feel right, trust your instincts and remove yourself from the situation. Costa Ricans are generally friendly and helpful, so if you encounter any issues, seek assistance from locals or law enforcement.

11. Purchase Travel Insurance: Consider getting comprehensive travel insurance that covers medical emergencies, trip cancellations, and lost belongings. This can provide peace of mind in case of unexpected situations.

12. Respect the Environment: Be mindful of the natural surroundings and wildlife. Follow local regulations, such as not feeding wild animals, to ensure both your safety and the preservation of Costa Rica's unique ecosystems.

Costa Rica is a wonderful destination for solo travelers, with its stunning landscapes, friendly people, and vibrant culture. By taking these safety considerations into account and staying vigilant, you can fully enjoy your solo adventure in this enchanting country.

3.3 Best Destinations for Solo Travelers

Costa Rica is a paradise for solo travelers seeking adventure, culture, and natural beauty. The country's warm hospitality and diverse landscapes make it an ideal destination for those exploring on their own. Here are some of the best destinations for solo travelers in Costa Rica:

1. San José:
   The capital city, San José, serves as an excellent starting point for your solo adventure. Explore the vibrant culture at the National Theater, visit museums, and sample local cuisine in its numerous markets. San José is a hub for transportation, making it easy to access other parts of the country.

2. La Fortuna:
   Nestled near the Arenal Volcano, La Fortuna is a mecca for adventure seekers. You can hike through lush rainforests, soak in natural hot springs, and

take on thrilling activities like zip-lining and white-water rafting. The friendly atmosphere and communal vibe of La Fortuna make it easy to connect with fellow travelers.

3. Monteverde:
   Monteverde's cloud forests are a solo traveler's dream. Explore hanging bridges, spot rare wildlife, and take part in guided night walks to witness the jungle come alive. The local eco-conscious community is welcoming, and there are plenty of group tours to join.

4. Puerto Viejo:
   On the Caribbean coast, Puerto Viejo offers a relaxed, bohemian vibe. Solo travelers can unwind on stunning beaches, explore the vibrant town, and immerse themselves in Afro-Caribbean culture. It's a great place to meet fellow travelers at beachside bars and hostels.

5. Manuel Antonio:
   For nature lovers, Manuel Antonio National Park is a must-visit. The park is a tropical paradise with lush rainforests and pristine beaches. Solo travelers can explore the park's many trails, where encounters with monkeys, sloths, and vibrant bird species are common.

6. Tamarindo:

If you're looking for a mix of beach life and nightlife, Tamarindo is your spot. This popular surf town offers solo travelers the chance to ride the waves, enjoy beachfront yoga classes, and socialize in the many bars and restaurants.

7. Osa Peninsula:

For a more off-the-beaten-path experience, head to the Osa Peninsula. It's a remote and wild region known for its incredible biodiversity. Solo travelers can explore Corcovado National Park, go whale-watching, and relax on untouched beaches.

8. Santa Teresa:

This laid-back beach town is perfect for solo travelers seeking a surfer's paradise. Santa Teresa offers consistent waves, yoga retreats, and a friendly, international community.

9. Guanacaste:

The Guanacaste province is known for its beautiful beaches and dry tropical forests. Solo travelers can take part in horseback riding, water sports, and explore Rincon de la Vieja National Park, known for its geothermal wonders.

10. Arenal Region:

The Arenal region is an excellent choice for solo travelers interested in photography, hiking, and relaxation. The iconic Arenal Volcano and the serene Lake Arenal provide breathtaking backdrops for your adventures.

Costa Rica's diverse landscapes and welcoming atmosphere make it an unforgettable destination for solo travelers. Whether you're seeking thrilling adventures or tranquil relaxation, you'll find plenty of opportunities to connect with fellow travelers and embrace the Pura Vida lifestyle.

3.4 Meeting Locals and Other Travelers

One of the most enriching aspects of solo travel in Costa Rica is the opportunity to connect with both locals and fellow travelers. Costa Ricans, often referred to as "Ticos" and "Ticas," are known for their warm and friendly nature, making it relatively easy to engage with them. Here are some tips and suggestions on how solo travelers can meet and interact with locals and other travelers in Costa Rica:

1. Learn Some Basic Spanish Phrases: While many Costa Ricans speak at least some English, having a few basic Spanish phrases in your repertoire can go

a long way in breaking the ice and showing respect for the local culture.

2. Stay in Local Accommodations: Consider staying in guesthouses, small hotels, or family-run lodges where you're more likely to interact with local hosts and other travelers. These places often provide a cozier and more communal atmosphere.

3. Join Group Activities: Participating in group tours and activities is a fantastic way to meet fellow travelers who share your interests. Whether it's a guided hike through a rainforest or a group surf lesson, these experiences foster a sense of camaraderie.

4. Attend Local Events: Keep an eye out for local events, festivals, and markets. These gatherings provide a glimpse into Costa Rican culture and offer the perfect opportunity to engage with locals. Try traditional food, dance to local music, and strike up conversations with vendors.

5. Explore Local Cafes and Restaurants: Visit local cafes and eateries frequented by Costa Ricans. Strike up conversations with the staff and patrons, and you might just discover hidden gems and gain valuable insights into the region.

6. Volunteer Opportunities: Many travelers find fulfillment in volunteering during their stay. There are numerous eco-friendly and community-based projects in Costa Rica that welcome volunteers. This not only allows you to make a positive impact but also connect with locals and like-minded travelers.

7. Use Social Media and Apps: Connect with other travelers in advance or during your trip through travel-related social media groups and apps. You can find fellow solo travelers, get recommendations, and even arrange meetups.

8. Be Approachable and Open: Solo travelers often find that simply being approachable and open to conversation leads to unexpected friendships. Smile, ask questions, and show genuine interest in the people you meet.

9. Respect Local Customs: Costa Ricans appreciate visitors who respect their customs and traditions. Politeness and a willingness to learn about the local way of life can lead to meaningful interactions.

Meeting locals and fellow travelers can transform your solo adventure in Costa Rica into a vibrant, culturally rich experience. It's these connections that often create lasting memories and provide a deeper understanding of the beautiful country and its people. So, don't be afraid to step out of your comfort zone and embrace the opportunity to connect with the wonderful individuals you'll encounter on your journey.

Chapter 4. Traveling with Kids

4.1 Family-Friendly Activities

Costa Rica is a paradise for families seeking adventure, nature, and cultural experiences. With its lush rainforests, stunning coastlines, and vibrant communities, this Central American gem offers a wide range of family-friendly activities that will leave lasting memories for both kids and adults.

1. Wildlife Encounters
Costa Rica is famous for its remarkable biodiversity. Take your family to the numerous wildlife reserves and national parks to witness the wonders of the animal kingdom. Children will be enthralled by the sight of playful monkeys, colorful

toucans, and the iconic three-toed sloths. Don't miss a visit to the renowned Tortuguero National Park to observe sea turtles nesting (seasonal).

2. Rainforest Adventures
Explore the rainforests on thrilling canopy tours. Zip-lining through the treetops, walking across hanging bridges, and taking guided nature hikes offer exciting opportunities for your family to get up close and personal with the tropical flora and fauna.

3. Beach Fun
Costa Rica boasts pristine beaches on both the Pacific and Caribbean coasts. Enjoy family-friendly beach activities such as building sandcastles, swimming, and boogie boarding. The gentle waves on many beaches make them ideal for children. Look for beaches with tide pools where little ones can discover fascinating marine life.

4. Volcano Exploration
Visiting the Arenal Volcano is a captivating experience for all ages. Take a guided tour to learn about the volcano's history and geology. Afterward, relax in one of the natural hot springs in the area, perfect for unwinding as a family.

5. Waterfalls and Swimming Holes

Discover the hidden gems of Costa Rica by hiking to beautiful waterfalls and swimming holes. These refreshing oases provide the perfect setting for picnics and swimming, and many are located in family-friendly national parks like Rincon de la Vieja.

6. Cultural Immersion
Teach your children about different cultures by visiting indigenous communities like the Bribrí or Boruca. Participate in cultural demonstrations, witness traditional dances, and shop for handmade crafts. These encounters offer valuable lessons and unforgettable experiences.

7. Adventure Parks
Costa Rica is home to various adventure parks that are perfect for families. Consider places like Diamante Eco Adventure Park or Hacienda Guachipelín Adventure Center, where you can enjoy a mix of thrilling activities, including zip-lines, horseback riding, and river tubing.

8. Butterfly Gardens and Wildlife Sanctuaries
Children will be captivated by the colorful butterflies at the butterfly gardens, such as the Butterfly Conservatory in Monteverde. Wildlife sanctuaries, like the Jaguar Rescue Center in Puerto

Viejo, offer educational opportunities for kids while they learn about conservation efforts.

9. Educational Tours
Plan visits to eco-educational centers, such as the Monteverde Frog Pond, where kids can learn about amphibians and reptiles. The Children's Eternal Rainforest in Monteverde and the La Paz Waterfall Gardens near San Jose also offer educational trails and wildlife exhibits.

Costa Rica's family-friendly activities provide the perfect blend of education, adventure, and relaxation, ensuring that your family creates unforgettable memories in this enchanting country. Whether you're exploring the rainforest, relaxing on the beach, or discovering the local culture, Costa Rica offers something for every member of the family to enjoy.

4.2 Child-Friendly Accommodations

When traveling to Costa Rica with your family, choosing child-friendly accommodations can make all the difference in ensuring a comfortable and memorable trip. Costa Rica offers a wide range of family-friendly lodging options that cater to both parents and kids. Here are some recommendations for child-friendly accommodations in various regions of Costa Rica:

1. Beachfront Resorts

- Tamarindo: Tamarindo is a popular beach town on the Pacific coast of Costa Rica and offers several family-friendly resorts. The Westin Playa Conchal Resort is known for its all-inclusive options and kid's club, providing various activities and services for children while parents enjoy the beautiful beach and amenities.

- Guanacaste: This region offers numerous beachfront resorts like the Dreams Las Mareas Resort and Spa. With spacious family suites and an Explorer's Club for kids, it's a great choice for families.

2. Eco-Lodges in the Rainforest

- Arenal: The Arenal area is perfect for families looking to explore the rainforest. The Arenal Observatory Lodge offers both adventure and comfort. Kids can enjoy guided nature tours and horseback riding while parents relax in natural hot springs.

- Manuel Antonio: This national park is a fantastic destination for wildlife enthusiasts. Consider staying at the Tulemar Bungalows, which provide private bungalows nestled in the jungle with access to their own beach. The family-sized accommodations and wildlife right outside your door make it a favorite for families.

3. Vacation Rentals

- Jaco: For a more relaxed beach vibe with easy access to amenities, consider renting a beachfront villa or condo in Jaco. There are many options available, and it's a great base for exploring the Central Pacific region.

- Tortuguero: Tortuguero is a unique destination, accessible only by boat or small plane. Consider renting a comfortable jungle lodge for a real adventure. Kids will love the boat tours through the canals, wildlife spotting, and the turtle nesting season.

4. All-Inclusive Family Resorts

- Papagayo Peninsula: The Planet Hollywood Beach Resort in Papagayo offers an all-inclusive experience with a kids' club, a variety of dining options, and fun activities for children. It's an excellent choice for a stress-free family vacation.

- Playa Conchal: The Reserva Conchal Beach Resort, Golf & Spa is another all-inclusive option with spacious family suites and an array of amenities, including a beautiful beach and a kids' club.

When booking accommodations, make sure to inquire about family-specific amenities, such as babysitting services, children's menus, and play areas. Costa Rica is a country that welcomes families with open arms, and these child-friendly accommodations will help make your family's visit to this beautiful country both enjoyable and memorable.

4.3 Safety Tips for Kids

Traveling with children in Costa Rica can be a wonderful and enriching experience. However, it's essential to prioritize safety to ensure a memorable and worry-free trip. Here are some safety tips for families with kids exploring the beauty of Costa Rica:

1. Sun Protection: The tropical sun in Costa Rica can be intense. Ensure that your children are

equipped with sunscreen, hats, and sunglasses to protect them from harmful UV rays. Apply sunscreen regularly, especially when spending time at the beach or in the mountains.

2. Insect Safety: Costa Rica is home to various insects, including mosquitoes. Bring insect repellent to shield your kids from bug bites. In some areas, consider using mosquito nets while sleeping.

3. Water Safety: If you plan on enjoying the country's beautiful beaches and rivers, keep a close eye on your children, especially if they're not strong swimmers. Ensure they have appropriate floatation devices and teach them about the importance of respecting the water.

4. Wildlife Awareness: Teach your children about Costa Rica's unique wildlife. While it's exciting to encounter animals, some can be dangerous. Keep a safe distance from wildlife, don't feed them, and follow the guidance of park rangers and tour guides.

5. Health Precautions: Prior to your trip, consult a healthcare professional about vaccinations and necessary medications. It's a good idea to have a

basic first-aid kit on hand, including any essential medications your child may need.

6. Safe Transportation: Whether you're using a rental car, public transportation, or taxis, ensure your child is securely fastened in an age-appropriate car seat or booster seat. Costa Rican roads can be winding and unpredictable, so prioritize their safety while traveling.

7. Local Food and Water: While Costa Rican cuisine is delicious, be cautious about street food and tap water. Stick to bottled water and eat at reputable restaurants to avoid foodborne illnesses that can be a concern, especially for kids.

8. Language and Communication: Teach your children some basic Spanish phrases, like "hello," "thank you," and "help." This can be both fun and useful for them to interact with locals and seek assistance if needed.

9. Emergency Contacts: Make sure your children know how to dial local emergency numbers, like 911, and how to reach the nearest embassy or consulate in case of any issues.

10. Exploration Together: Encourage your children to explore with you, not alone. The country's diverse landscapes and ecosystems are breathtaking but can also be challenging. Hiking, nature walks, and adventure activities are great for family bonding.

11. Respect Local Customs: Teach your kids about the importance of respecting local customs and cultures. This includes dressing modestly in certain areas and being mindful of cultural traditions and expectations.

12. Stay Informed: Stay updated on current travel advisories and local news. Awareness of any potential risks or natural disasters can help you make informed decisions for your family's safety.

By following these safety tips and being vigilant, you can ensure that your family's adventure in Costa Rica is not only enjoyable but also secure. Costa Rica offers a wealth of enriching experiences for kids and adults alike, making it an ideal destination for family travel.

4.4 Educational Opportunities for Children

Costa Rica is not only a land of natural wonders but also a place where learning opportunities abound. Families traveling with children will find a wealth of educational experiences waiting to enrich their understanding of the world. From wildlife encounters to cultural immersion, Costa Rica offers a variety of educational activities for kids of all ages.

1. Wildlife Exploration:

Costa Rica's astounding biodiversity provides an excellent opportunity for children to learn about the natural world. National parks and wildlife reserves like Manuel Antonio National Park and Tortuguero National Park offer guided tours that teach kids about the country's diverse ecosystems, conservation efforts, and fascinating species like sloths, toucans, and sea turtles.

2. Butterfly and Hummingbird Gardens:

Butterfly and hummingbird gardens, such as La Paz Waterfall Gardens and Monteverde Butterfly Gardens, offer an up-close look at these captivating creatures. Children can witness the metamorphosis of butterflies and the extraordinary flight patterns of hummingbirds while gaining insights into their crucial roles in the ecosystem.

3. Rainforest Canopy Tours:

Zip-lining through the rainforest canopy is an exciting adventure that also provides valuable lessons in ecology. Many tour operators emphasize the importance of forest preservation and the role of the canopy in housing various species. This thrilling activity doubles as an educational experience.

4. Indigenous Communities:

Visiting indigenous communities, like the BriBri or Boruca, offers a unique cultural learning opportunity for children. They can interact with local children, learn about traditional crafts, and gain insight into the cultural heritage and sustainable living practices of Costa Rica's indigenous people.

5. Language and Cultural Experiences:

Enrolling children in language schools, where they can learn Spanish, is an excellent educational option. Additionally, exploring local markets, tasting traditional cuisine, and participating in traditional dance or music workshops offer cultural immersion that broadens their horizons.

6. Sea Turtle Conservation:

Costa Rica is renowned for its sea turtle nesting sites. Participating in night patrols with conservation organizations in places like Tortuguero provides children with a unique opportunity to learn about these endangered species and the conservation efforts to protect them.

7. Volunteering Opportunities:
Many organizations in Costa Rica offer family-friendly volunteer experiences. Families can contribute to reforestation projects, wildlife rescue centers, or beach clean-up initiatives, allowing children to actively engage in environmental conservation efforts.

8. Interactive Museums:
Costa Rica boasts interactive museums, like the Children's Museum (Museo de los Niños) in San José, designed to engage and educate children on a wide range of topics, including science, history, and culture.

Costa Rica's commitment to education and sustainability, combined with its breathtaking natural beauty, makes it an ideal destination for families seeking to provide their children with enriching and educational travel experiences. From exploring the rainforest to engaging with local communities, the opportunities for learning and growth are endless in this beautiful Central American country.

Chapter 5. Couples' Getaway

5.1 Romantic Experiences in Costa Rica

Costa Rica is not just a paradise for nature enthusiasts; it's also a dream destination for couples seeking a romantic getaway. From lush rainforests to pristine beaches, this Central American gem offers a myriad of romantic experiences. Here are some of the most enchanting moments you can share with your loved one in Costa Rica:

1. Sunset at Manuel Antonio: Witnessing a Pacific sunset from the golden sands of Manuel Antonio Beach is a magical experience. As the sun dips below the horizon, the sky transforms into a canvas of vibrant colors, providing the perfect backdrop for a romantic stroll.

2. Arenal Hot Springs: Nestled at the base of the Arenal Volcano, you'll find natural hot springs that are a delight for couples. Soak in the warm, mineral-rich waters and enjoy the soothing ambiance as you gaze at the stars above.

3. Beachfront Dinners: Many coastal restaurants in Costa Rica offer beachfront dining, allowing you to savor fresh seafood and local cuisine while listening to the soothing sound of the waves. It's an ideal setting for a romantic candlelit dinner.

4. Canopy Walks in Monteverde: Walk hand in hand along the canopy bridges of Monteverde Cloud Forest. The breathtaking views, diverse flora, and the thrill of being surrounded by nature make it a unique and memorable experience.

5. Romantic Wildlife Encounters: The diverse wildlife of Costa Rica offers fascinating opportunities for bonding. Spotting colorful toucans, playful monkeys, or elusive sloths in their natural habitats is an adventure you won't forget.

6. Waterfall Rappelling: For adventurous couples, rappelling down a jungle waterfall can be an exhilarating and bonding experience. Many tour

operators in Costa Rica offer this adrenaline-pumping adventure amidst stunning natural surroundings.

7. Boat Tours in Tortuguero: Take a tranquil boat tour through the meandering waterways of Tortuguero National Park. You might spot nesting sea turtles, exotic birds, and lush vegetation, all while sharing the serenity of the moment.

8. Private Villas and Bungalows: Choose to stay in a secluded jungle bungalow or a private villa overlooking the ocean. Costa Rica offers a range of romantic accommodations where you can enjoy intimacy and privacy.

9. Horseback Riding on the Beach: Explore pristine, deserted beaches on horseback with your partner. It's a romantic way to experience the unspoiled beauty of Costa Rica's coastlines.

10. Sunrise in Drake Bay: Wake up early to witness the first rays of the sun painting the sky over Drake Bay. It's a tranquil and awe-inspiring moment that will stay with you long after you leave.

Costa Rica's romantic experiences are as diverse as its landscapes. Whether you're seeking adventure or quiet moments together, this tropical paradise has something for every couple looking to create unforgettable memories of their journey.

5.2 Adults-Only Resorts

Costa Rica is not only known for its stunning natural beauty but also for its adults-only resorts that offer a tranquil and romantic escape for couples, honeymooners, and adults seeking a peaceful vacation. These resorts are designed to cater to your every need, providing a serene atmosphere and a range of amenities. Here are some top recommendations:

1. Secrets Papagayo Costa Rica:
   - Located in the Gulf of Papagayo, this luxurious adults-only resort offers stunning views of the Pacific Ocean and a secluded beach.
   - All-inclusive packages cover gourmet dining, top-shelf drinks, and various activities, including snorkeling and yoga.
   - The resort features a world-class spa and well-appointed suites with private terraces or swim-out access.

2. Nayara Springs:

- Nestled in the Arenal Volcano National Park, Nayara Springs is an intimate, boutique resort for adults.
- Stay in your own secluded villa with a private plunge pool and outdoor shower.
- Enjoy natural hot springs, lush rainforest surroundings, and exceptional dining options.

3. El Mangroove, Autograph Collection:
- Situated in the Papagayo Bay, this chic adults-only resort boasts modern design and direct access to the beach.
- The resort offers an array of water sports, a spa, and exceptional dining options.
- Its location provides the perfect base for exploring the nearby national parks and wildlife.

4. Tabacon Grand Spa Thermal Resort:
- Famous for its natural hot springs, Tabacon is a luxury resort located at the base of the Arenal Volcano.
- Indulge in thermal spa treatments, relax in the thermal pools, and explore the lush rainforest surroundings.
- The resort offers privacy and comfort in a serene environment.

5. Harmony Hotel:

- Harmony Hotel in Nosara is an eco-friendly, adults-only boutique hotel that combines luxury with sustainability.
- The property is surrounded by lush gardens and is just steps from Playa Guiones, a world-renowned surfing beach.
- Enjoy yoga sessions, spa treatments, and farm-to-table dining.

6. Alma Del Pacifico Beach Hotel & Spa:
- This beachfront boutique hotel offers a peaceful retreat in Esterillos Este.
- Stay in colorful villas inspired by Costa Rican art and design.
- Relax by the pool, indulge in spa treatments, and savor exquisite coastal cuisine.

These adults-only resorts in Costa Rica offer an ideal setting for a romantic and tranquil vacation, where you can unwind, explore the beauty of the country, and create unforgettable memories with your partner. Whether it's a honeymoon, anniversary, or just a getaway for two, these resorts provide the perfect backdrop for a romantic escape.

5.3 Adventure Activities for Couples

Costa Rica, with its lush rainforests, rugged mountains, and pristine coastlines, is a paradise for adventurous couples seeking a thrilling escape. Whether you're newlyweds on a honeymoon or simply looking to ignite that spark of adventure, there's no shortage of adrenaline-pumping activities to enjoy together. Here are some of the top adventure activities for couples in Costa Rica:

1. Zip-Lining through the Canopy:

Soar above the rainforest canopy hand in hand as you experience the exhilarating rush of zip-lining. Costa Rica boasts numerous zip-line tours, with platforms and lines strategically placed to provide breathtaking views of the jungle below. The sensation of gliding through the treetops with your loved one is sure to create unforgettable memories.

2. Whitewater Rafting:

Challenge yourselves with a whitewater rafting expedition on Costa Rica's pristine rivers. Whether you're beginners or experienced rafters, there are options for all skill levels. Share the excitement of navigating thrilling rapids as you bond amidst the untamed beauty of the country's waterways.

3. Horseback Riding on the Beach:

For a romantic adventure, consider a horseback ride along the coastline at sunset. The feeling of the warm sea breeze and the rhythmic sound of hoofbeats in the sand as you explore secluded beaches is nothing short of magical.

4. ATV Tours:
   Explore the rugged terrains of Costa Rica's countryside together on an ATV adventure. These tours take you through winding trails, forests, and even volcanic landscapes, offering a unique and thrilling way to connect with nature.

5. Scuba Diving and Snorkeling:
   Discover the vibrant underwater world of Costa Rica by embarking on a scuba diving or snorkeling excursion. Share the wonder of exploring coral reefs and encountering colorful marine life while exploring the Pacific and Caribbean coastlines.

6. Canyoning and Waterfall Rappelling:
   Descend deep into the heart of the rainforest and face your fears together with canyoning and waterfall rappelling. Experienced guides will lead you through lush canyons, making your way down cascading waterfalls – an adventure that combines adrenaline with the stunning beauty of nature.

7. Caving and Spelunking:
   Venture into the underground realm of Costa Rica's caves and caverns. Couples can explore the

subterranean wonders and learn about the geological history while experiencing a sense of mystery and wonder together.

8. Nighttime Wildlife Safaris:

Embrace the thrill of the night with a guided wildlife safari in one of Costa Rica's renowned national parks. Encounter the country's diverse nocturnal inhabitants, from bats to owls and elusive jungle cats.

9. Hot Air Balloon Rides:

For a more serene yet enchanting adventure, consider a hot air balloon ride over Costa Rica's incredible landscapes. Soar above volcanoes, forests, and valleys, all while sharing the beauty of the moment with your partner.

10. Paragliding and Hang Gliding:

Experience the ultimate feeling of freedom as you glide through the skies together in a tandem paraglider or hang glider. The bird's-eye views of Costa Rica's natural wonders are truly awe-inspiring.

Costa Rica's thrilling adventure activities provide the perfect backdrop for couples to strengthen their bond while creating lasting memories. Whether you're seeking an adrenaline rush, a tranquil escape, or a blend of both, this vibrant country has something for every adventurous duo to enjoy.

5.4 Dining and Nightlife for Two

Costa Rica is not only known for its breathtaking natural beauty and outdoor adventures but also for its vibrant dining and nightlife scene. Whether you're a couple seeking a romantic evening or just looking to enjoy the local flavors, Costa Rica has something to offer to satisfy every palate and create lasting memories.

Dining Experiences for Two:

1. Beachfront Dining: One of the most romantic dining experiences can be found at beachfront restaurants, where you can savor delicious seafood while listening to the sound of the waves. Popular beach destinations like Tamarindo and Manuel Antonio offer a range of options.

2. Farm-to-Table Delights: Costa Rica is known for its fresh and organic produce. Enjoy farm-to-table dining in restaurants that source their ingredients locally, creating a delightful and sustainable culinary experience.

3. Candlelit Dinners: Many restaurants offer intimate, candlelit dinners, perfect for couples. These settings create a cozy and romantic atmosphere for an unforgettable evening.

4. Costa Rican Cuisine: Don't miss the opportunity to savor authentic Costa Rican dishes such as "casado" (a typical plate with rice, beans, meat, and plantains) or "ceviche" (a refreshing seafood dish). Explore the local flavors and enjoy the country's culinary heritage.

Nightlife for Two:

1. Salsa Dancing: Enjoy a night of dancing in Costa Rica's salsa clubs. Whether you're experienced dancers or just looking to have fun, you'll find lively salsa clubs in San Jose and other major cities.

2. Live Music: Costa Rica offers a variety of live music venues, from reggae to Latin rhythms. Check local listings for live bands or artists performing during your stay.

3. Casinos: If you're feeling lucky, try your hand at one of the country's casinos. They offer a thrilling and glamorous night out for couples looking for excitement.

4. Beach Bars: For a more laid-back evening, beach bars along the coast provide a relaxing setting to enjoy cocktails, listen to live music, and watch the sunset over the Pacific or Caribbean.

5. Craft Cocktails: Many bars and lounges in Costa Rica offer craft cocktails made with exotic local ingredients. Explore the creativity of Costa Rican mixologists and enjoy unique drinks with your loved one.

Costa Rica's dining and nightlife scene is as diverse as its natural landscapes. Whether you prefer a romantic dinner under the stars or dancing the night away, you'll find plenty of options to create unforgettable moments as a couple. So, raise a toast to your Costa Rican adventure and make the most of the country's delicious cuisine and vibrant nightlife.

Chapter 6. Planning Your Itinerary

6.1 Sample Itineraries

When planning your trip to Costa Rica, having a well-structured itinerary can help you make the most of your visit. Here, we've crafted three sample itineraries to cater to the diverse interests of travelers, whether you're adventuring solo, exploring with your family, or embarking on a romantic getaway with your partner.

6.1.1 Solo Traveler's Itinerary

Day 1: San Jose Arrival
- Arrive in San Jose, the capital of Costa Rica.
- Explore the city's cultural gems, including the National Theater and Central Market.

- Enjoy local cuisine at a traditional "soda."

Day 2: Arenal Adventure
- Head to Arenal Volcano National Park for hiking and hot springs.
- Visit the Arenal Observatory Lodge for incredible volcano views.
- Relax in the natural thermal pools.

Day 3: Monteverde Cloud Forest
- Transfer to the Monteverde Cloud Forest Reserve.
- Go ziplining or explore hanging bridges through the canopy.
- Discover unique flora and fauna in the cloud forest.

Day 4: Manuel Antonio's Beaches
- Travel to Manuel Antonio National Park on the Pacific coast.
- Explore the park's diverse wildlife and relax on pristine beaches.
- Choose from various water activities like kayaking and snorkeling.

Day 5: Surf's Up in Tamarindo
- Drive to Tamarindo on the Nicoya Peninsula.
- Catch some waves with a surf lesson or simply soak up the beach vibes.

- Tamarindo offers vibrant nightlife for solo travelers.

Day 6: Guanacaste Adventure
- Experience adventure activities like ATV tours or horseback riding.
- Discover the natural beauty of Guanacaste's landscapes.
- End the day with a sunset cocktail on the beach.

Day 7: Return to San Jose
- Head back to San Jose for your departure.
- Spend your last day souvenir shopping or visiting any missed attractions.
- Bid farewell to Costa Rica with a heart full of memories.

6.1.2 Family-Friendly Itinerary

Day 1: Arrival in San Jose
- Arrive in San Jose and check into family-friendly accommodations.
- Get acquainted with the city's culture by visiting museums and parks.

Day 2: La Paz Waterfall Gardens
- Explore La Paz Waterfall Gardens, a kid-friendly nature park.

- Visit the butterfly observatory and observe rescued wildlife.
- Enjoy the stunning waterfalls and hiking trails.

Day 3: Arenal and Hot Springs
- Transfer to Arenal for family adventures.
- Hike in the Arenal Volcano National Park.
- Relax in natural hot springs suitable for all ages.

Day 4: Hanging Bridges in Monteverde
- Discover the Monteverde Cloud Forest via hanging bridges.
- Take a guided nature walk to spot colorful birds and mammals.
- Enjoy the vibrant ecosystem.

Day 5: Manuel Antonio's Wildlife
- Travel to Manuel Antonio National Park.
- Join a guided tour to spot monkeys, sloths, and exotic birds.
- Spend family time on beautiful beaches.

Day 6: Marine Fun in Tortuguero
- Reach Tortuguero on the Caribbean coast.
- Go on a boat tour to explore the canals and spot wildlife.
- Learn about sea turtles in the village.

Day 7: Return to San Jose
- Return to San Jose for departure.
- Reflect on the family's Costa Rican adventure before heading home.

6.1.3 Couples' Romantic Getaway

Day 1: Romantic Welcome in San Jose
- Begin your romantic journey with a cozy stay in San Jose.
- Explore the charming streets and dine at a romantic restaurant.

Day 2: Arenal's Volcanic Romance
- Travel to Arenal, known for its natural beauty.
- Relax in hot springs with stunning volcano views.
- Enjoy a romantic dinner overlooking Arenal Lake.

Day 3: Monteverde's Enchanted Forest
- Transfer to Monteverde and experience the cloud forest's magic.
- Take a night walk to admire nocturnal creatures.
- Share a private, candlelit dinner.

Day 4: Beachside Bliss in Manuel Antonio
- Head to Manuel Antonio for romantic beach days.
- Relax on pristine beaches and take a sunset stroll.

- Book a couple's massage or enjoy a private beachfront dinner.

Day 5: Adventure and Love in Tamarindo
- Travel to Tamarindo for adventure and romance.
- Explore the natural beauty of Guanacaste together.
- Share a thrilling experience, like a sunset catamaran cruise.

Day 6: Secluded Moments in Uvita
- Reach Uvita on the South Pacific coast.
- Discover the secluded beauty of Uvita Beach and its famous "Whale's Tail."
- Spend quality time together in a tranquil environment.

Day 7: Farewell to Costa Rica
- Return to San Jose for your departure.
- Savor one last romantic meal before leaving Costa Rica with cherished memories.

These sample itineraries offer a glimpse of the countless experiences that await travelers in Costa Rica, whether you're solo, with family, or on a romantic escape. Tailor your journey to your preferences and create memories that will last a lifetime.

6.2 Must-See Destinations

Costa Rica is a country blessed with natural beauty, diverse ecosystems, and a rich cultural heritage. Exploring this small but captivating nation is an adventure in itself. Here, we highlight some of the must-see destinations that will make your Costa Rica trip truly unforgettable.

1. Arenal Volcano: Arenal is one of Costa Rica's most iconic volcanoes, and the surrounding area is a paradise for nature lovers and adventure seekers. You can soak in natural hot springs, hike the Arenal Volcano National Park, and enjoy thrilling activities like ziplining and hanging bridge tours.

2. Manuel Antonio National Park: This coastal gem is known for its stunning beaches and diverse wildlife. Hike through lush rainforests, relax on pristine beaches, and keep an eye out for sloths, monkeys, and exotic birds.

3. Monteverde Cloud Forest: Monteverde is a haven for cloud forest explorers. The mystical cloud forests are home to a remarkable variety of flora and fauna. Don't miss the opportunity to take a canopy tour through the treetops or walk along suspension bridges for a unique perspective.

4. Tortuguero National Park: Located on the Caribbean coast, Tortuguero is famous for its nesting sea turtles, including the green sea turtle. Witnessing a sea turtle nesting or hatching is a mesmerizing experience. Guided boat tours through the park's canals offer excellent wildlife viewing opportunities.

5. Corcovado National Park: Known as "the most biologically intense place on Earth" by National Geographic, Corcovado is a remote wilderness area teeming with biodiversity. Hiking here may lead to encounters with jaguars, tapirs, and scarlet macaws.

6. Osa Peninsula: The Osa Peninsula offers pristine rainforests, rugged coastlines, and untouched beaches. It's an ideal destination for adventure and wildlife enthusiasts, with numerous hiking and birdwatching opportunities.

7. Guanacaste Province: Guanacaste is famous for its beautiful beaches, vibrant culture, and dry tropical forests. It's the place to go for sun and surf, with popular destinations like Tamarindo and Playa Conchal.

8. Puerto Viejo de Talamanca: Located on the Caribbean coast, Puerto Viejo is a laid-back town known for its reggae vibe and stunning beaches. Explore the Cahuita National Park, enjoy water sports, and savor delicious Caribbean cuisine.

9. San Jose: Costa Rica's capital city is often overlooked, but it has its own charm. Explore the National Museum, visit the Gold Museum, and wander through the bustling Central Market to get a taste of Costa Rican urban life.

10. La Fortuna Waterfall: Located near Arenal, this majestic waterfall is a postcard-worthy natural wonder. Hike to the base of the waterfall and take a refreshing dip in its cool waters.

These must-see destinations in Costa Rica offer a wide range of experiences, from outdoor adventures and wildlife encounters to cultural exploration and relaxation on pristine beaches. Whether you're a solo traveler, a family with kids, or a couple seeking a romantic getaway, these destinations have something special to offer, making your Costa Rica journey an unforgettable one.

6.3 Off-the-Beaten-Path Adventures

Costa Rica is a country of incredible diversity, offering travelers more than just the well-trodden tourist paths. For those seeking a truly unique and off-the-beaten-path experience, there are numerous hidden gems waiting to be discovered. Here, we delve into some of the lesser-known, yet equally enchanting, aspects of this stunning destination.

1. Remote Rainforests and Waterfalls:
   Venture beyond the popular national parks and explore remote rainforests where the sounds of nature dominate. Seek out hidden waterfalls tucked away in lush, green landscapes. Take a guided tour or hike independently, and you'll be rewarded with pristine natural beauty, untouched by the crowds.

2. Indigenous Encounters:
   Discover the rich culture of Costa Rica's indigenous communities. Travel to places like Bribri, the home of the Bribri and Cabecar tribes. Engage with local artisans, learn about their traditions, and sample indigenous cuisine for a unique cultural immersion.

3. Hidden Beaches on the Pacific and Caribbean Coasts:

While Costa Rica is famous for its beaches, there are hidden stretches of coastline that remain tranquil and unspoiled. Explore the hidden coves and secluded shores, like Playa Conchal on the Pacific coast or Punta Uva on the Caribbean side, for a quieter and more intimate beach experience.

4. Volcanic Hot Springs Off the Grid:
   While many tourists flock to La Fortuna and the Arenal Volcano, lesser-known volcanic areas like Rincon de la Vieja offer stunning geothermal hot springs experiences without the crowds. Soak in natural pools surrounded by volcanic landscapes, often tucked away in remote locations.

5. Underrated National Parks:
   Beyond the famous parks like Manuel Antonio and Corcovado, consider visiting lesser-known parks like Santa Rosa National Park in Guanacaste, where you can explore dry tropical forests and historical sites. This can provide a unique opportunity to connect with nature and history in a more serene setting.

6. River Expeditions:
   While white-water rafting and kayaking are popular, consider off-the-beaten-path river expeditions. The Rio Savegre on the Pacific coast

offers thrilling rapids amid breathtaking rainforest scenery and is a well-kept secret among adventure seekers.

7. Wildlife Sanctuaries:

Costa Rica is celebrated for its biodiversity, but some lesser-known wildlife sanctuaries offer up-close encounters with rescued or rehabilitated animals. Places like the Alturas Wildlife Sanctuary provide a chance to see animals like sloths, monkeys, and toucans while supporting conservation efforts.

8. Agricultural Tourism:

Explore the agricultural side of Costa Rica by visiting lesser-known coffee and chocolate farms. You can learn about the cultivation and processing of these beloved products and savor the flavors of local crops away from the tourist crowds.

Costa Rica's off-the-beaten-path experiences promise an authentic and intimate connection with the country's natural wonders, diverse culture, and hidden treasures. By veering away from the mainstream tourist routes, travelers can create lasting memories and unique stories to share. Embrace the adventure and discover the real essence of this extraordinary Central American destination.

Chapter 7. Getting Around Costa Rica

Costa Rica is a diverse and beautiful country, and to truly explore its wonders, you'll need to know how to get around. Whether you prefer flexibility in your own vehicle, an adventurous road trip, or a more eco-friendly public transportation experience, Costa Rica has options to suit your travel style.

7.1 Transportation Options

Costa Rica offers a variety of transportation options to cater to different preferences and budgets. Here are the main methods of getting around:

- Car Rentals: Renting a car is a popular choice for tourists seeking flexibility and the ability to reach remote destinations. There are various rental agencies at major airports and cities. Be sure to choose a 4x4 vehicle if you plan to venture off the beaten path.

- Domestic Flights: If you're looking to save time and cover long distances quickly, consider domestic flights. Costa Rica has several regional airports connecting popular tourist destinations.

- Shuttle Services: Shared shuttle services are convenient for traveling between major tourist destinations. They provide a comfortable, door-to-door experience, which is ideal for families or groups.

- Taxis: Taxis are readily available in cities and towns. They are a convenient way to explore local areas, but make sure to agree on the fare before starting your ride.

- Buses: Costa Rica's public bus system is extensive and cost-effective. While it may not be the fastest option, it's an excellent choice for budget travelers.

Long-distance buses are comfortable and equipped with air conditioning.

7.2 Car Rentals and Driving Tips

Renting a car in Costa Rica can be a great way to explore the country at your own pace. However, it's essential to be aware of some tips and guidelines for a smooth driving experience:

- Driving Conditions: Roads in Costa Rica can vary from well-paved highways to bumpy dirt tracks. It's advisable to choose a 4x4 vehicle, especially if you plan to explore remote areas or visit during the rainy season.

- Navigation: GPS can be extremely helpful, but it's wise to carry physical maps as well. Some rural areas may have limited or no GPS signal.

- Traffic Rules: Costa Rica follows standard traffic rules, including driving on the right side of the road. Seat belts are mandatory, and the legal blood alcohol limit is low, so it's best not to drink and drive.

- Road Signs: Familiarize yourself with road signs, as they may be in Spanish. Knowing common Spanish traffic terms is beneficial.

- Fuel: Gas stations are widespread, but it's a good practice to keep your tank reasonably full, especially when driving in remote areas.

7.3 Public Transportation

Costa Rica's public transportation system is efficient, affordable, and eco-friendly. Here's what you need to know about using public transportation:

- Buses: Public buses are the most common means of transportation in Costa Rica. They serve cities, towns, and even some remote areas. Bus fares are economical, making it an excellent choice for budget travelers.

- Trains: While Costa Rica's train system is limited, it's an enjoyable way to explore the countryside, particularly the Pacific coast. The scenic routes provide a unique perspective of the country's natural beauty.

- Ferries: If you're traveling to destinations like the Nicoya Peninsula, you may need to take a ferry. These short boat trips provide a scenic and refreshing break in your journey.

- San José's City Buses: In the capital city, San José, you can efficiently navigate using the city's extensive public bus system. These buses are an economical way to explore the city and its surroundings.

In summary, getting around Costa Rica offers a range of transportation options, each with its advantages. Whether you prefer the independence of a rental car, the adventure of public buses, or the speed of domestic flights, Costa Rica's diverse landscape can be explored with ease, ensuring that you make the most of your Costa Rican adventure.

Chapter 8. Accommodations

8.1 Hotels and Resorts

Costa Rica is renowned for its breathtaking natural beauty and vibrant culture, making it a dream destination for travelers from around the world. To fully immerse yourself in this tropical paradise, choosing the right accommodations is essential. Whether you're a solo adventurer, a family with kids, or a couple seeking a romantic escape, Costa Rica offers a diverse range of hotels and resorts to suit every preference and budget. Here are some recommendations for various types of travelers:

1. Solo Travelers:

- Selina Hostels: With locations across Costa Rica, Selina Hostels provide a welcoming atmosphere for solo travelers. These hostels offer a blend of comfortable dormitories and private rooms, making them ideal for those seeking social interactions and activities.

- Peace Lodge: Nestled in the heart of the La Paz Waterfall Gardens Nature Park, Peace Lodge offers a serene environment for solo travelers who desire a peaceful retreat. It's a great place to connect with nature.

2. Families with Kids:

- Tabacón Thermal Resort & Spa: Located near Arenal Volcano, Tabacón offers a unique family-friendly experience. Its hot springs, lush gardens, and adventure activities make it perfect for kids and adults alike.

- JW Marriott Guanacaste Resort & Spa: Families looking for a luxurious beachfront stay will appreciate the JW Marriott's amenities, including a Kids Club and a championship golf course.

3. Couples:

- Nayara Springs: This adults-only boutique resort in the Arenal Volcano area provides a romantic atmosphere with private plunge pools and lush rainforest surroundings.

- Arenas del Mar Beachfront and Rainforest Resort: For a romantic beachside retreat, consider Arenas del Mar in Manuel Antonio. It offers stunning ocean views and easy access to a pristine beach.

4. Budget Travelers:

- Hostel Pangea: Situated in the heart of San Jose, Hostel Pangea is a budget-friendly option with a lively social scene, ideal for travelers on a tight budget.

- Cabinas Las Olas: Located in Puerto Viejo, Cabinas Las Olas provides affordable accommodation near the beach, perfect for those looking to experience the Caribbean coast without breaking the bank.

5. Luxury Seekers:

- Four Seasons Resort Costa Rica at Peninsula Papagayo: As one of the most prestigious resorts in the country, the Four Seasons offers luxury and privacy in a pristine setting.

- Andaz Costa Rica Resort at Peninsula Papagayo: This high-end resort combines contemporary design with natural beauty, providing a luxurious escape on the Papagayo Peninsula.

6. Eco-Lovers:

- Lapa Rios Ecolodge: Lapa Rios is an eco-lodge set within a private rainforest reserve on the Osa Peninsula. It's the perfect choice for those who want to immerse themselves in nature and support sustainable tourism.

- Finca Rosa Blanca Coffee Plantation & Inn: This eco-friendly boutique hotel near San Jose focuses on sustainable agriculture and offers a unique coffee farm experience.

Remember to book your accommodations well in advance, especially during peak travel seasons, and consider your preferences and travel style when choosing the perfect place to stay in Costa Rica. Whether you're seeking adventure, relaxation, or a mix of both, Costa Rica's hotels and resorts have you covered.

8.2 Vacation Rentals

When planning a trip to Costa Rica, one of the most important decisions you'll make is where to stay. While the country boasts a wide range of accommodations, from luxury resorts to eco-lodges, vacation rentals are an increasingly popular and versatile option for travelers.

Why Choose Vacation Rentals?

Vacation rentals in Costa Rica offer a unique and personalized experience, making them an attractive choice for a variety of travelers, including families, couples, and solo adventurers. Here are some compelling reasons to consider vacation rentals:

1. Space and Comfort: Vacation rentals provide more space than traditional hotel rooms, often including multiple bedrooms, living areas, and fully equipped kitchens. This extra room is especially beneficial for families traveling with children or groups of friends.

2. Privacy: Many vacation rentals are secluded and offer a level of privacy that's hard to find in crowded resorts. Enjoy your own piece of paradise, whether it's a beachfront villa, a rainforest cabin, or a mountain retreat.

3. Cost-Efficiency: If you're traveling with a group, the cost per person can be significantly lower than booking individual hotel rooms. Additionally, having a kitchen allows you to prepare your meals, saving on dining expenses.

4. Local Experience: Staying in a vacation rental allows you to immerse yourself in the local culture. You'll often be located in residential neighborhoods or off the beaten path, giving you a more authentic experience of Costa Rica.

5. Flexibility: Vacation rentals offer more flexible check-in and check-out times, which can be a boon for travelers with varying schedules. You can set your own pace and enjoy the freedom to come and go as you please.

Types of Vacation Rentals

Costa Rica offers a wide range of vacation rental options to suit various preferences and budgets. Here are some popular types of vacation rentals in the country:

1. Beachfront Villas: Wake up to the sound of the ocean in a private beachfront villa. These luxurious

rentals often come with pools and direct access to the beach.

2. Jungle Cabins: For a true rainforest experience, consider staying in a jungle cabin. These accommodations immerse you in the heart of Costa Rica's lush biodiversity.

3. Mountain Retreats: If you're seeking cooler climates and stunning mountain views, mountain retreat vacation rentals provide a peaceful escape.

4. City Apartments: In bustling cities like San José, you can find modern and comfortable apartment rentals close to cultural attractions and vibrant neighborhoods.

5. Eco-Friendly Lodges: Costa Rica is renowned for its commitment to sustainability. Many eco-friendly vacation rentals blend seamlessly with the natural environment.

Booking Vacation Rentals

Booking vacation rentals in Costa Rica is made easy through various online platforms and local rental agencies. It's advisable to book well in advance, especially during the peak travel seasons. Before finalizing your rental, consider factors like location, amenities, and reviews to ensure it meets your specific needs.

Vacation rentals in Costa Rica provide an excellent way to experience the country on your terms, whether you're looking for relaxation, adventure, or a blend of both. With the right rental, you'll create cherished memories and enjoy the pura vida lifestyle of this stunning Central American destination.

8.3 Camping and Glamping

Costa Rica's lush and diverse natural beauty beckons outdoor enthusiasts to experience the thrill of camping and the comfort of glamping within its pristine landscapes. Whether you prefer roughing it in a tent under a starry sky or relishing the luxuries of a well-appointed safari-style tent, Costa Rica has options to suit all tastes.

Camping in Costa Rica:

1. National Parks and Reserves: Many of Costa Rica's national parks and wildlife reserves offer camping facilities. Camping enthusiasts can find designated campgrounds with basic amenities such as restrooms, showers, and picnic areas. Popular

parks like Manuel Antonio and Santa Rosa provide the opportunity to immerse yourself in nature.

2. Beachside Camping: For an unforgettable experience, consider beachside camping along the Pacific or Caribbean coasts. Picture waking up to the sound of crashing waves and taking in breathtaking sunsets over the ocean. Playa Hermosa, Santa Teresa, and Cahuita are some of the coastal gems known for camping.

3. Volcano Camping: Camping near one of Costa Rica's active volcanoes, such as Arenal or Rincon de la Vieja, offers a unique adventure. You can enjoy hikes through volcanic landscapes, relaxing in natural hot springs, and observing the fascinating geothermal activity.

4. Remote Wilderness Camping: If you seek true solitude, venture into the country's remote wilderness areas. Remote camping might require more self-sufficiency, as facilities are limited, but it allows you to connect with Costa Rica's untamed nature.

5. Camping Essentials: When camping in Costa Rica, be sure to bring essential gear, including a reliable tent, sleeping bags, insect repellent, and a

first-aid kit. Respect the Leave No Trace principles to preserve the natural environment.

Glamping in Costa Rica:

1. Luxury Tent Camps: Glamping, a blend of "glamorous" and "camping," offers an extravagant camping experience. In Costa Rica, you can find luxury tent camps nestled in the heart of the rainforest or overlooking the Pacific Ocean. These well-appointed tents often come with comfortable beds, en-suite bathrooms, and sometimes even air conditioning.

2. Eco-Friendly Glamping: Costa Rica places a strong emphasis on eco-tourism, and many glamping sites follow suit. Eco-friendly glamping resorts are designed to minimize their environmental impact, with sustainable practices such as solar power, composting, and organic dining.

3. Wildlife-Inspired Retreats: Some glamping sites are built to complement Costa Rica's rich biodiversity. Imagine staying in a treehouse-style tent where you can spot monkeys, sloths, and colorful birds right from your porch. These

accommodations provide a truly immersive experience in the jungle.

4. Glamping by the Beach: For a more romantic or tranquil escape, beachfront glamping resorts offer the ideal setting. Wake up to the sound of the waves, take long walks along the sandy shores, and enjoy the beauty of Costa Rica's coastlines.

Camping and glamping in Costa Rica cater to a wide range of travelers, from rugged adventurers to those seeking a touch of luxury. Whichever experience you choose, you'll find yourself surrounded by the country's incredible biodiversity and unforgettable natural landscapes. Make sure to plan ahead and book your camping or glamping experience in advance, as these options are popular among tourists looking to connect with Costa Rica's unparalleled wilderness.

Chapter 9. Dining and Cuisine

9.1 Costa Rican Food Overview

Costa Rican cuisine is a flavorful reflection of the country's rich cultural heritage and the abundance of fresh ingredients available from its fertile lands and surrounding waters. Known for its simplicity and reliance on staples like rice and beans, Costa Rican food offers a delightful array of tastes that cater to various palates. Here's an overview of the essential elements of Costa Rican cuisine:

1. Gallo Pinto: This iconic dish is a daily staple, combining rice and beans sautéed with onions, peppers, and spices. It's often served as a side dish with eggs, cheese, or meat and is the quintessential Costa Rican breakfast.

2. Casados: These are hearty, traditional lunchtime plates that typically include rice, beans, a protein (such as chicken, beef, or fish), and accompanying sides like plantains, salad, and picadillo (a vegetable hash).

3. Plantains: A beloved ingredient, plantains are often fried until crispy and served alongside many dishes. Tostones (twice-fried plantains) and maduros (sweet, ripe plantains) offer delightful variations.

4. Seafood: With both Pacific and Caribbean coastlines, Costa Rica offers a bounty of fresh seafood. You'll find ceviche, a zesty seafood salad, and various fish dishes prepared with tropical ingredients.

5. Tamal: These savory delights consist of masa (corn dough) filled with meat, vegetables, and spices, then wrapped in a banana leaf and steamed.

Tamales are a traditional treat, often enjoyed during festivals and holidays.

6. Olla de Carne: A hearty beef soup brimming with vegetables and root crops, olla de carne is a favorite comfort food, especially in the cooler mountainous regions.

7. Chifrijo: A popular bar snack, chifrijo combines crispy chicharrón (pork cracklings) with black beans, pico de gallo, and avocado. It's a flavorful and satisfying appetizer.

8. Salsa Lizano: This ubiquitous condiment is found on almost every Costa Rican table. It's a tangy, slightly sweet sauce that enhances the flavor of various dishes, including gallo pinto.

9. Coffee: Costa Rica is renowned for its high-quality coffee. A visit to a local café, known as a "soda," is a must for coffee enthusiasts. Pair your coffee with traditional pastries like empanadas or rosquillas (cornmeal cookies).

10. Desserts: Satisfy your sweet tooth with treats like tres leches cake, flan, or arroz con leche (rice pudding).

Costa Rican food emphasizes fresh and locally sourced ingredients, making it a culinary journey that connects you to the heart of the country. Be sure to explore the local markets and sodas to experience the authentic flavors of Costa Rica during your visit.

9.2 Local Dishes to Try

Costa Rica is not only renowned for its stunning natural landscapes but also for its vibrant and flavorful cuisine. As you explore this beautiful country, don't miss the opportunity to indulge in a diverse range of local dishes that offer a unique culinary experience. Here are some of the must-try local dishes in Costa Rica:

1. Gallo Pinto: Considered the national dish of Costa Rica, Gallo Pinto is a hearty and delicious combination of rice and black beans. It's often mixed with cilantro, onions, and bell peppers, and served as a side dish for breakfast, lunch, or dinner.

2. Casado: This traditional Costa Rican dish is a well-balanced meal consisting of rice, black beans, plantains, a choice of meat (such as chicken, beef, or fish), and a side salad. Casado offers a taste of local flavors with a variety of textures and flavors on one plate.

3. Arroz con Pollo: A flavorful and comforting dish, Arroz con Pollo is a chicken and rice casserole cooked in a savory tomato-based sauce. It's often seasoned with achiote, a spice that gives the dish its distinctive orange color.

4. Olla de Carne: A hearty Costa Rican soup, Olla de Carne features a rich beef broth filled with chunks of beef, vegetables like yuca, corn, and plantains. It's a warm and satisfying dish, perfect for cooler days.

5. Ceviche: As Costa Rica boasts a long coastline, fresh seafood is a culinary treasure. Ceviche is a popular choice – it's made by marinating raw fish or seafood in lime juice and mixing it with onions, cilantro, and bell peppers. The acidity of the lime juice "cooks" the fish, resulting in a zesty and refreshing appetizer.

6. Tamales: Tamales are a traditional dish made from corn masa (dough) filled with a variety of ingredients like chicken, vegetables, or cheese, then wrapped in banana leaves and steamed. Tamales are often enjoyed during special occasions and holidays.

7. Chifrijo: A delicious and satisfying snack, Chifrijo is a combination of crispy fried pork pieces (chicharrones), black beans, diced tomatoes, and a sprinkle of Lizano sauce. It's typically served with tortilla chips for dipping.

8. Picadillo: This flavorful and aromatic dish features ground beef cooked with a mix of vegetables, including bell peppers, peas, and potatoes. It's seasoned with various spices and served with rice. It's a favorite comfort food for many Costa Ricans.

9. Tamal Asado: Different from the traditional tamale, Tamal Asado is a grilled version. The corn masa is grilled until it becomes slightly crispy, offering a unique texture and taste.

10. Rondón: If you find yourself on the Caribbean coast of Costa Rica, don't miss trying Rondón. It's a hearty coconut stew that combines seafood, plantains, yams, and various vegetables in a rich coconut milk broth.

When exploring Costa Rica, sampling these local dishes is a delightful way to immerse yourself in the country's culture and savor the authentic flavors of this enchanting destination. Whether you're a food enthusiast or simply looking for a culinary adventure, Costa Rica's cuisine is sure to leave a lasting impression on your taste buds.

9.3 Dietary Options and Restrictions

Costa Rica, with its rich and diverse culinary traditions, offers a variety of dietary options to cater to the needs of travelers with different preferences and dietary restrictions. Whether you're a vegetarian, vegan, or have specific food allergies, you can navigate the country's food scene with relative ease.

1. Vegetarian and Vegan Choices:
   Costa Rica is welcoming to vegetarians and vegans. Many restaurants and eateries offer meat-free options, and you'll find dishes featuring fresh vegetables, beans, rice, and tropical fruits. Common vegetarian dishes include "casado" (rice and beans with plantains) and "gallo pinto" (rice and beans). Vegans can enjoy these dishes without dairy products, and many places serve tofu and soy-based products as meat substitutes.

2. Gluten-Free Dining:
   If you have a gluten intolerance or celiac disease, you can still enjoy Costa Rican cuisine. Corn is a staple ingredient, so dishes like corn tortillas and

"tamales" are typically gluten-free. However, it's essential to communicate your dietary needs clearly at restaurants to avoid cross-contamination.

3. Food Allergies and Dietary Restrictions:
   Travelers with food allergies should take precautions when dining out. It's advisable to learn basic Spanish phrases to communicate your allergies to restaurant staff. Costa Ricans are generally understanding and accommodating, but it's essential to be vigilant. Carry allergy cards written in Spanish to explain your dietary restrictions.

4. Fresh Fruits and Vegetables:
   Costa Rica's abundance of fresh fruits and vegetables makes it an ideal destination for health-conscious travelers. You can savor an array of tropical fruits like mangoes, papayas, pineapples, and coconuts. These make for delicious snacks and breakfast options.

5. Seafood Delights:
   Costa Rica's coastal regions offer a bounty of fresh seafood. If you're a pescatarian, you're in for a treat. Indulge in dishes like "ceviche" (marinated raw fish or seafood), "arroz con camarones" (shrimp with rice), and a variety of fish preparations.

6. Cultural Sensitivity:
   While exploring local markets and street food, you might come across exotic dishes like fried insects. While these are part of the culinary culture, they may not suit everyone's tastes. Be open to trying new things, but also know your limits.

7. International Cuisine:
   In addition to traditional Costa Rican dishes, you'll find a wide range of international cuisines in major cities and tourist areas. Italian, Chinese, and American fast food are readily available. This diversity ensures that even picky eaters will find something to enjoy.

Remember that Costa Rican cuisine is often prepared with a focus on natural, locally sourced ingredients. It's essential to communicate your dietary needs clearly and be flexible when dining in more remote areas. By doing so, you can enjoy the delicious flavors of Costa Rica while adhering to your dietary preferences and restrictions.

Chapter 10. Adventure and Outdoor Activities

10.1 Hiking and Nature Walks

Costa Rica's stunning natural beauty and diverse landscapes make it a paradise for hikers and nature enthusiasts. From lush rainforests to active volcanoes and pristine beaches, the country offers a wide array of hiking and nature walk experiences that cater to travelers of all levels of expertise. Whether you're a seasoned trekker or just looking for a leisurely stroll, Costa Rica has something to offer you.

Diverse Trails and Ecosystems: Costa Rica's varied geography provides a rich tapestry of hiking opportunities. The country boasts tropical rainforests, cloud forests, coastal trails, and volcanic terrains, each with its unique flora and fauna. One moment you can find yourself traversing dense jungles teeming with wildlife, and the next, you might be ascending a volcano to witness breathtaking panoramic views.

Monteverde Cloud Forest Reserve: One of the country's most famous hiking destinations is the Monteverde Cloud Forest Reserve. This misty, mystical forest is home to a mind-boggling variety of plants, animals, and birds, including the resplendent quetzal. There are trails suited for all levels of hikers, making it an excellent family adventure.

Arenal Volcano National Park: For those seeking an adrenaline rush, the Arenal Volcano National Park offers challenging hikes with the chance to witness lava flows and volcanic activity. The surrounding rainforests are filled with wildlife, and hot springs provide a soothing post-hike relaxation option.

Manuel Antonio National Park: On the Pacific coast, Manuel Antonio National Park offers relatively easy trails through lush rainforests and ends at pristine beaches. Capuchin monkeys, sloths, and a variety of tropical birds are common sights along the way, making it an excellent option for wildlife enthusiasts.

Corcovado National Park: Serious trekkers and wilderness lovers won't want to miss Corcovado National Park. It's one of the most biologically diverse places on Earth, boasting a vast network of trails through primary rainforests. Tapirs, jaguars, and scarlet macaws are just a few of the park's inhabitants.

Guided Tours and Self-Guided Hikes: Costa Rica offers both guided hiking tours led by experienced naturalists and self-guided options for independent travelers. Guided tours provide in-depth knowledge of the local ecosystems and wildlife, while self-guided hikes allow for more flexibility and solitude.

Safety and Conservation: It's essential to respect the natural environment and adhere to park rules to minimize your impact on these pristine areas. Stay on marked trails, pack out all trash, and be cautious of the wildlife, especially in more remote areas.

Many national parks have entrance fees that contribute to their conservation efforts.

Hiking and nature walks in Costa Rica offer an immersive and authentic way to experience the country's stunning landscapes and remarkable biodiversity. Whether you're seeking adventure, relaxation, or a deeper connection with nature, the trails of Costa Rica are waiting to be explored, making it a must-do activity for any traveler visiting this ecological wonderland.

10.2 Zip-Lining and Canopy Tours

Costa Rica's lush rainforests and diverse landscapes offer travelers the perfect playground for thrilling adventures, and one of the most popular ways to experience the country's natural beauty is through zip-lining and canopy tours. This exhilarating activity allows visitors to glide through the treetops, soaring above the forest canopy and taking in breathtaking vistas. Here's everything you need to know about zip-lining and canopy tours in Costa Rica.

What Are Zip-Lining and Canopy Tours?

Zip-lining and canopy tours are outdoor recreational activities that involve traveling along a suspended cable from one platform to another, typically high above the ground. In Costa Rica, these tours provide a unique opportunity to explore the rainforest from a bird's-eye perspective. Platforms are strategically placed within the forest, connected by cables, and participants are securely harnessed to a pulley system, ensuring safety while they glide through the trees.

Why Choose Costa Rica for Zip-Lining and Canopy Tours?

Costa Rica is renowned for its pristine rainforests and rich biodiversity, making it an ideal setting for zip-lining and canopy tours. The country offers a wide range of zip-line experiences, from short and family-friendly tours to adrenaline-pumping adventures that traverse deep into the heart of the jungle. The unique combination of adrenaline and nature exploration sets Costa Rica apart as a premier destination for this activity.

Best Locations for Zip-Lining and Canopy Tours

1. Monteverde: The cloud forests of Monteverde are famous for their diverse flora and fauna. Here, you can embark on thrilling canopy tours that allow you

to glide through the misty forest, spotting rare species along the way.

2. Arenal: In the shadow of the majestic Arenal Volcano, zip-lining tours offer panoramic views of the volcano, lush rainforests, and pristine lakes.

3. Manuel Antonio: Combining beach and jungle, Manuel Antonio's canopy tours offer a unique experience where you can spot both monkeys and macaws while soaring above the canopy.

4. Guanacaste: In this region, you can enjoy zip-lining over dry tropical forests, creating a striking contrast to the verdant rainforests commonly associated with Costa Rica.

Tips for Zip-Lining and Canopy Tours

- Dress appropriately: Wear comfortable clothing and closed-toe shoes. Long shorts or pants are recommended to prevent harness discomfort.

- Listen to your guide: Follow the instructions of the trained guides who will ensure your safety throughout the tour.

- Capture the moment: Most tour operators provide photo and video services, so you can relive the experience later.

- Choose tours based on your comfort level: There are various options, including slower-paced tours suitable for families and more intense experiences for adrenaline junkies.

- Respect the environment: Remember that you are guests in the rainforest. Avoid littering, and follow sustainable tourism practices.

Zip-lining and canopy tours in Costa Rica offer a unique perspective on the country's stunning natural beauty. Whether you're seeking an adrenaline rush or a serene journey through the treetops, these tours promise an unforgettable adventure in the heart of the rainforest.

10.3 Water Sports: Surfing, Snorkeling, and Diving

Costa Rica, with its stunning coastlines along both the Pacific Ocean and the Caribbean Sea, offers a paradise for water sports enthusiasts. Whether you're an adrenaline junkie seeking thrilling waves or a leisurely snorkeler exploring vibrant marine life, Costa Rica has something for everyone. Here's a closer look at the exciting world of surfing, snorkeling, and diving in this tropical haven.

Surfing: Riding the Pacific Swells

Costa Rica is renowned for its world-class surf spots that cater to all skill levels. The Pacific coast, in particular, is a surfer's dream come true. The region of Guanacaste offers a mix of powerful beach breaks and gentle, rolling waves. Tamarindo and Playa Grande are popular choices for surfers of all abilities, while the famous Witch's Rock stands as a challenge for the pros.

For those looking for a more remote and serene experience, the Nicoya Peninsula is home to hidden gems like Santa Teresa and Mal Pais. These beaches provide a quieter atmosphere and excellent surf conditions.

On the Caribbean side, Puerto Viejo and Cahuita offer a unique Caribbean flair and mellow waves. Surfing here is a relaxed and culturally immersive experience.

Snorkeling: Exploring Underwater Beauty

Costa Rica boasts diverse marine life, and snorkeling is a fantastic way to witness the underwater wonders. The clear waters around the Cano Island Biological Reserve, located off the Osa Peninsula, provide a vibrant snorkeling experience. Here, you can encounter colorful coral reefs, sea turtles, rays, and an array of tropical fish.

The Cahuita National Park, on the Caribbean coast, features a coral reef close to the shore, making it easily accessible for snorkelers. The protected marine area ensures an up-close encounter with parrotfish, angelfish, and sea urchins in their natural habitat.

Diving: Descending into the Deep

For scuba diving enthusiasts, Costa Rica offers an opportunity to explore the world beneath the waves. Cocos Island, a UNESCO World Heritage Site, is a remote and exhilarating dive location. It's famous for hammerhead shark sightings, giant manta rays, and schools of fish in the midst of a pristine underwater environment.

The Bat Islands, part of the Guanacaste region, are another favorite for experienced divers, providing a chance to encounter bull sharks, rays, and massive schools of fish.

On the Caribbean coast, the Gandoca-Manzanillo Wildlife Refuge showcases a different side of Costa Rica's marine life, with colorful coral formations and diverse fish species. This area is ideal for both novice and experienced divers.

When engaging in water sports, always prioritize safety. Many areas in Costa Rica have local surf schools, snorkeling tours, and diving centers with experienced guides who can assist and ensure your adventures are enjoyable and secure.

Whether you're riding the waves, exploring coral reefs, or diving with sharks, the water sports in Costa Rica are sure to create unforgettable memories, making your trip an aquatic adventure of a lifetime.

10.4 Wildlife Viewing

Costa Rica, known as the "Rich Coast," is a haven for wildlife enthusiasts. This Central American gem boasts an astonishing variety of ecosystems, making it one of the world's most biodiverse destinations. Whether you're a solo traveler, a family with kids, or a couple seeking a unique experience, wildlife viewing in Costa Rica is a must-include activity on your itinerary.

Diverse Habitats: Costa Rica's geographical diversity is astounding. From pristine beaches and lush rainforests to towering mountains and volcanic landscapes, the country's diverse habitats are home to an incredible array of wildlife. Whether you're exploring the dense rainforests of Corcovado National Park, the high-altitude cloud forests of Monteverde, or the wetlands of Tortuguero, you'll encounter a vast range of species in their natural environments.

Iconic Wildlife: Costa Rica is famous for its "big five" wildlife species: jaguars, pumas, sloths, sea turtles, and quetzals. Sloths, in particular, are often considered the country's unofficial mascot. Their leisurely movements through the treetops are a common sight, making them a favorite subject for wildlife photographers. The national parks and reserves offer opportunities to spot elusive big cats like jaguars and pumas, especially during guided night tours.

Birdwatchers' Paradise: For bird enthusiasts, Costa Rica is a paradise with over 900 bird species, including the resplendent quetzal, toucans, and scarlet macaws. Monteverde's cloud forest and the Osa Peninsula are prime spots for birdwatching. Joining a local guide or naturalist will enhance your chances of spotting rare and colorful avian species.

Marine Marvels: Don't forget the marine life! Costa Rica's Pacific and Caribbean coasts are rich in marine biodiversity. Embark on a snorkeling or diving adventure and swim alongside sea turtles, colorful coral reefs, and a diverse array of fish. Whale-watching tours offer a chance to witness humpback and pilot whales, along with playful dolphins.

Ethical Wildlife Encounters: Responsible tourism is essential in Costa Rica. Choose tour operators and guides who prioritize ethical wildlife encounters. For example, sea turtle nesting tours in Tortuguero or Ostional are conducted with strict conservation guidelines to protect these endangered creatures. Respect the natural habitats and maintain a safe distance from wildlife to ensure their well-being and preservation.

Best Times for Wildlife Viewing: The dry season (December to April) is ideal for wildlife viewing as animals are more active. However, the wet season (May to November) also has its perks, as it's the time when turtles nest, frogs and insects are more active, and landscapes are lush and green.

Tips for Wildlife Enthusiasts:
- Invest in a quality pair of binoculars and a good camera to capture wildlife moments.
- Hire local guides who possess expert knowledge of the area and its wildlife.
- Be patient and allow for quiet observation to spot elusive creatures.
- Respect park rules and regulations, such as staying on designated trails and maintaining a low impact on the environment.

Costa Rica's natural beauty and incredible wildlife make it a must-visit destination for those who have a deep appreciation for the natural world. Whether you're observing sloths in the rainforest, tracking jaguars through the jungle, or marveling at the vibrant plumage of toucans, your wildlife viewing adventures in Costa Rica will leave you with memories to last a lifetime.

Chapter 11. Culture and History

11.1 Costa Rican Culture

Costa Rica's culture is as diverse and vibrant as its breathtaking landscapes. As you embark on your journey through this enchanting country, take some time to immerse yourself in the rich tapestry of Costa Rican culture, which is a harmonious blend of indigenous heritage, Spanish influences, and a strong sense of community and environmental stewardship.

Pura Vida: The Essence of Costa Rican Life
"Pura Vida" is a phrase you'll hear throughout your Costa Rican adventure. It's more than just a saying;

it's a way of life. This expression translates to "pure life" and encapsulates the Tico spirit of simplicity, happiness, and contentment. Costa Ricans are known for their warm and welcoming nature, and they take pride in living a life filled with gratitude and optimism. Visitors will often find themselves infected with the Pura Vida spirit, which is a reminder to appreciate life's simple pleasures.

Family and Community Values
Costa Ricans hold strong family bonds and a deep sense of community close to their hearts. Extended families often live in the same neighborhoods, and gatherings, festivals, and religious celebrations are important occasions for socializing. Respect for elders and a strong commitment to family values are integral parts of the culture. These values are reflected in the warm and welcoming attitude of the locals, making Costa Rica an inviting destination for travelers of all kinds.

Festivals and Celebrations
Costa Rica boasts a calendar full of vibrant festivals and celebrations. The most famous is the Independence Day parade on September 15th, where towns across the country come alive with music, dancing, and colorful parades. Additionally, many towns have their own unique festivals, such

as the Palmares Festival, the Fiestas de Zapote, and the Oxcart Parade in San Jose. These events provide an excellent opportunity to experience local traditions and immerse yourself in the festive spirit of Costa Rica.

Indigenous Roots and Influence
Before the Spanish arrived in the 16th century, Costa Rica was inhabited by indigenous peoples such as the Bribri, Cabécar, and Boruca. Although their numbers have decreased, their cultural influence remains. You can explore indigenous communities and learn about their traditions, artwork, and way of life, which are deeply connected to nature and the environment.

Music and Dance
Costa Rican music is a lively mix of African, European, and indigenous influences. Traditional instruments like marimbas, drums, and flutes are often used in folk music, while cumbia and salsa are popular dance forms. You'll find opportunities to enjoy live music and dance performances throughout your journey, offering an authentic taste of Costa Rican rhythms.

Culinary Traditions

Costa Rican cuisine reflects its agricultural heritage. Staples like rice and beans are combined to create the famous dish "gallo pinto," often served with a side of plantains and cheese. Fresh fruits, tropical juices, and seafood are abundant, and you'll want to savor the flavors of local markets, street vendors, and traditional restaurants. Coffee is also an essential part of Costa Rican culture, with the country renowned for producing some of the world's finest beans.

Environmental Stewardship
Costa Ricans are passionate about environmental conservation. The country is home to an astonishing array of biodiversity, and there's a deep commitment to preserving it. As a traveler, you can join in these efforts by participating in ecotourism activities and exploring the many national parks and wildlife reserves that Costa Rica offers.

In essence, Costa Rican culture is a celebration of life, nature, and community. It's an integral part of the country's allure, making it a destination that offers not only stunning natural beauty but also a cultural experience that's as warm and welcoming as its people. Embrace the Pura Vida spirit, connect with locals, and savor the rich tapestry of traditions that define Costa Rica's unique culture.

11.2 Indigenous Communities

Costa Rica is not only known for its stunning natural beauty but also for its rich cultural diversity. One of the integral components of this cultural tapestry is the presence of indigenous communities. These communities have inhabited the region for centuries, preserving their traditions and way of life amidst the ever-changing world.

Diversity of Indigenous Peoples:
Costa Rica is home to eight indigenous groups, each with its own unique language, customs, and practices. These groups include the Bribri, Cabécar, Maleku, Bribrís, Borucas, Ngäbe, Buglere, and the Teribe/Térraba. Each community contributes to the country's cultural mosaic and offers a glimpse into the indigenous heritage of Costa Rica.

Traditional Lifestyles:
These indigenous communities maintain strong connections to the land and live in harmony with nature. Their traditional way of life revolves around agriculture, where they cultivate crops like cacao, bananas, and root vegetables. Many still reside in thatched-roof huts and practice age-old customs passed down through generations.

Unique Arts and Crafts:

The indigenous communities of Costa Rica are renowned for their exceptional craftsmanship. You can find intricate handmade crafts, such as woven baskets, masks, and intricate pottery. These items often feature vibrant colors and intricate designs, making them unique souvenirs for travelers.

Cultural Experiences:
Visiting indigenous communities can be a profoundly enriching experience for travelers. Many communities welcome tourists and offer guided tours, allowing you to learn about their way of life, traditions, and the vital role they play in preserving Costa Rica's natural and cultural heritage.

Eco-Tourism and Conservation:
Indigenous communities are often located in ecologically significant areas, and many have taken up the cause of environmental conservation. They are stewards of the land, and their deep connection to nature has led to the protection of valuable ecosystems. As a visitor, you can participate in eco-tourism activities, such as nature walks and wildlife observation, guided by community members.

Respect and Ethical Tourism:

When visiting indigenous communities, it's essential to do so respectfully and ethically. Respect their customs and traditions, seek permission before taking photographs, and support their local economy by purchasing handmade crafts and products.

Exploring indigenous communities in Costa Rica is a unique opportunity to learn about the country's rich heritage, cultural diversity, and the vital role these communities play in preserving the environment. It's a chance to connect with people whose way of life is rooted in deep respect for the land, offering a meaningful and authentic experience for travelers.

11.3 Historical Sites

Costa Rica, often known for its lush rainforests and pristine beaches, also boasts a rich history that is well worth exploring during your visit. The country's history is shaped by indigenous cultures, Spanish colonization, and the struggle for independence. While Costa Rica may not have the towering pyramids of Egypt or the grandeur of European castles, its historical sites offer a glimpse into a unique and captivating past.

1. Cartago Ruins

- Located in Cartago, the former capital of Costa Rica, these ruins date back to the 16th century. The Cartago Ruins include the Santiago Apostol Parish Ruins and the Parroquia de Nuestra Señora de las Angustias Ruins. They are remnants of the original colonial churches and stand as a testament to the earthquakes that have shaken the region.

2. Orosi Church
- Nestled in the picturesque Orosi Valley, the Iglesia de San José de Orosi is the oldest church still in use in Costa Rica. Constructed in 1743, its beautiful colonial architecture and serene surroundings make it a must-visit historical site.

3. Guanacaste's Historical Park
- This park in the province of Guanacaste is a living testament to Costa Rica's cattle ranching history. It features preserved ranch buildings, a historic schoolhouse, and a traditional sugar mill, providing insight into the daily life of Costa Ricans in the 19th century.

4. Santa Rosa National Park
- Not only is Santa Rosa one of Costa Rica's oldest national parks, but it's also a historical site with immense significance. The Hacienda Santa Rosa, located within the park, was the site of the pivotal

Battle of Santa Rosa in 1856 during the country's fight for independence.

5. Museo Nacional (National Museum)
   - While not a historical site in the traditional sense, the Museo Nacional in San Jose is a treasure trove of Costa Rica's history and culture. Housed in an impressive former military barracks, the museum features a wide range of exhibits, from pre-Columbian artifacts to contemporary art.

6. Stone Spheres of the Diquís
   - The stone spheres of Costa Rica are a UNESCO World Heritage site and a historical mystery. These perfectly carved spheres are believed to have been created by the indigenous Diquís people over a thousand years ago. Their purpose and the methods used to create them remain topics of debate and intrigue.

Exploring these historical sites will not only give you a deeper appreciation for Costa Rica's past but also offer a chance to marvel at the country's natural beauty, as many of these sites are set against stunning landscapes. Whether you're interested in architecture, archaeology, or simply want to connect with the history of this remarkable country, Costa Rica's historical sites are sure to leave a lasting impression.

Chapter 12. Wildlife and Biodiversity

12.1 Unique Flora and Fauna

Costa Rica is renowned for its extraordinary biodiversity, making it a paradise for nature lovers. The country's diverse ecosystems, from lush rainforests to coastal mangroves and high-altitude cloud forests, provide a home to an astonishing array of unique flora and fauna. Here, you'll encounter some of the world's most fascinating and rare species.

*Flora:

1. Resplendent Orchids: Costa Rica is home to an astonishing variety of orchid species, including the national flower, the guaria blanca. Orchid enthusiasts will be captivated by the country's impressive orchid gardens and natural displays.

2. Giant Ferns: Some cloud forests in Costa Rica boast gigantic ferns that can reach up to 3 meters in height. These ferns create a magical, prehistoric atmosphere that is a must-see for visitors.

3. Butterfly-Friendly Plants: The country's gardens and reserves are adorned with plants that attract countless species of butterflies, adding vibrant colors to your nature walks.

*Fauna:

1. Scarlet Macaw: These strikingly colorful parrots can be spotted in various parts of Costa Rica, particularly in Corcovado National Park and the Osa Peninsula. Their loud calls and vivid plumage make them a must-see for bird enthusiasts.

2. Three-Toed Sloth: Costa Rica is home to both two-toed and three-toed sloths. These incredibly slow-moving creatures are often seen lounging in the treetops, making for an endearing sight.

3. Quetzal: The resplendent quetzal, with its emerald plumage and distinctive tail feathers, is a symbol of freedom and beauty. Birdwatchers often flock to Monteverde Cloud Forest Reserve to catch a glimpse of this elusive bird.

4. Red-Eyed Tree Frog: Known for its striking appearance, the red-eyed tree frog is an iconic Costa Rican species. They are most active at night, and their vibrant colors serve as a warning to potential predators.

5. Humpback Whales: Off the Pacific coast of Costa Rica, you can witness the incredible migration of humpback whales. These majestic marine giants make their journey here to breed and give birth, providing a spectacular natural spectacle.

6. Bats: Costa Rica is home to an impressive variety of bat species. Some caves and rainforest areas offer the opportunity to witness these nocturnal creatures up close during guided tours.

7. Poison Dart Frogs: These tiny yet brightly colored frogs are known for their toxic skin secretions. Costa Rica hosts various species of these

amphibians, which can be found in rainforests and protected reserves.

Costa Rica's unique flora and fauna provide an unparalleled opportunity to connect with the natural world. Whether you're a birdwatcher, a botanist, or just someone who appreciates the wonders of nature, Costa Rica's diverse ecosystems offer a remarkable journey through some of the most extraordinary and unique life forms on Earth.

12.2 Wildlife Reserves and National Parks

Costa Rica is renowned for its rich biodiversity, and one of the best ways to experience this natural wonderland is by exploring its wildlife reserves and national parks. These protected areas cover a significant portion of the country and provide sanctuary to a remarkable array of flora and fauna. Whether you're a nature enthusiast, an avid bird-watcher, or simply seeking a serene escape into the heart of the rainforest, Costa Rica's parks and reserves offer an unforgettable experience.

Manuel Antonio National Park
Located on the Pacific coast, Manuel Antonio National Park is one of Costa Rica's smallest yet most popular parks. It's famous for its white-faced capuchin monkeys, three-toed sloths, and a variety

of birds. The park's pristine beaches are perfect for a post-hike swim.

Tortuguero National Park
Situated on the Caribbean coast, Tortuguero National Park is a critical nesting site for endangered sea turtles, including green and leatherback turtles. Guided tours allow you to witness these incredible creatures laying their eggs.

Monteverde Cloud Forest Reserve
For a mystical experience, visit the Monteverde Cloud Forest Reserve. This misty and lush forest is home to a vast number of bird species, orchids, and unique mammals like the elusive quetzal.

Corcovado National Park
Corcovado, often called "the most biologically intense place on Earth," is located on the Osa Peninsula. It's a true wilderness experience, where jaguars, tapirs, and a plethora of rare species thrive.

Arenal Volcano National Park
Arenal Volcano National Park boasts stunning landscapes with the iconic Arenal Volcano as the centerpiece. Here, you can soak in hot springs, hike to lava fields, and witness the volcano's eruptions (from a safe distance).

Cahuita National Park
On the Caribbean coast, Cahuita National Park is known for its vibrant coral reefs and marine life. Snorkelers and divers will revel in the opportunity to explore these underwater wonders.

Rincon de la Vieja National Park
This park, named after the active Rincon de la Vieja Volcano, offers a diverse range of activities. Hike to see volcanic mud pots, waterfalls, and enjoy thermal hot springs.

When visiting these natural treasures, remember to follow ecotourism principles by respecting the environment, staying on designated paths, and leaving no trace. Additionally, hiring local guides can enhance your experience by providing insights into the unique ecosystems and wildlife.

Exploring Costa Rica's wildlife reserves and national parks is a profound way to connect with nature, appreciate the importance of conservation, and create lasting memories of your Costa Rican adventure. Don't forget your camera, binoculars, and a sense of wonder as you embark on these incredible journeys into the heart of Costa Rica's wilderness.

12.3 Bird-Watching

Costa Rica is a paradise for bird-watchers, offering a diverse and stunning array of avian species against the backdrop of lush tropical landscapes. With over 900 recorded bird species, this small Central American country is often considered one of the world's premier bird-watching destinations.

Rich Biodiversity: One of the key factors that make Costa Rica a haven for bird enthusiasts is its remarkable biodiversity. The country's varying elevations, from coastal regions to mountainous terrain, provide a wide range of habitats for birds. You can explore tropical rainforests, cloud forests, wetlands, and coastal ecosystems, each hosting unique birdlife.

Resplendent Birds: Bird-watchers can look forward to spotting a multitude of resplendent species. Among the most sought-after birds are the resplendent quetzal, known for its striking emerald and crimson plumage, and the harpy eagle, one of the world's largest and most powerful eagles. Costa Rica's national parks and wildlife reserves are excellent places to catch glimpses of these magnificent creatures.

Birding Hotspots: Costa Rica boasts several renowned bird-watching hotspots. The Monteverde Cloud Forest Reserve, situated at higher altitudes, is famous for its cloud forest species. Corcovado National Park, located on the Osa Peninsula, provides a chance to see rare and endemic birds. Tortuguero National Park along the Caribbean coast is home to waterfowl and herons, while Palo Verde National Park is a top destination for shorebirds.

Guided Tours: For those new to bird-watching or seeking a more immersive experience, guided tours are readily available. Knowledgeable local guides can help you identify and appreciate the rich birdlife of Costa Rica. They often possess a keen understanding of bird calls, making it easier to locate hidden avian treasures.

Timing Your Visit: Bird-watching is a year-round activity in Costa Rica, but the best time can vary by location and the species you want to see. The dry season, from December to April, is generally preferred for bird-watching as it provides clearer views and less rain.

Conservation Efforts: Costa Rica's dedication to environmental conservation ensures that bird habitats are preserved and protected. Many national parks and reserves are dedicated to the preservation of bird species and their ecosystems.

Photography Opportunities: Bird-watching in Costa Rica offers excellent opportunities for bird photography. Capture images of toucans, parrots, and hummingbirds against the vibrant backdrop of the country's natural beauty.

Travel Essentials: When planning a bird-watching trip to Costa Rica, be sure to invest in a good pair of binoculars, field guides, and a camera with a telephoto lens. Additionally, pack comfortable hiking gear, insect repellent, and rain gear for unexpected tropical showers.

Whether you're a seasoned birder or a beginner, the enchanting world of Costa Rican birds is sure to captivate you. With its unparalleled biodiversity and dedicated conservation efforts, Costa Rica promises an unforgettable bird-watching adventure for nature enthusiasts of all levels.

Chapter 13. Beaches and Coastlines

13.1 Pacific and Caribbean Beaches

Costa Rica, often called the "rich coast," is blessed with a diverse range of stunning beaches along its Pacific and Caribbean coasts. Each coast offers a unique beach experience, catering to different tastes and preferences.

Pacific Coast Beaches: Where Adventure Meets Serenity

The Pacific coast of Costa Rica is known for its vibrant surf culture, dramatic sunsets, and a plethora of adventure activities. Here, you'll find beaches to suit everyone from thrill-seekers to tranquil sunset admirers.

1. Tamarindo Beach: Located in the Guanacaste region, Tamarindo Beach is famous for its excellent surfing conditions. The long sandy stretch and lively atmosphere make it an ideal place to ride the waves or enjoy beachfront nightlife.

2. Manuel Antonio National Park: This pristine beach, nestled within the confines of a biodiverse national park, offers a unique blend of nature and relaxation. You can observe wildlife while swimming in the calm, turquoise waters.

3. Santa Teresa and Mal Pais: A haven for surfers and bohemian travelers, these neighboring beaches boast some of the best waves in the country. The rustic charm and laid-back vibe attract those looking to unwind and explore.

Caribbean Coast Beaches: Where Culture Meets Nature

The Caribbean coast of Costa Rica is an entirely different world, with a distinct Afro-Caribbean influence, lush rainforests, and diverse marine life.

This region offers a slower-paced, more cultural beach experience.

1. Puerto Viejo de Talamanca: This vibrant coastal town is a melting pot of cultures, featuring reggae beats, colorful Caribbean cuisine, and a relaxed atmosphere. Nearby beaches like Cocles and Punta Uva offer pristine white sands and excellent snorkeling opportunities.

2. Cahuita National Park: A hidden gem of the Caribbean coast, Cahuita National Park offers not only a beautiful beach but also an underwater wonderland for snorkelers. The coral reefs are teeming with marine life, making it a snorkeler's paradise.

3. Tortuguero: Known as the "Land of Turtles," this remote beach destination is famous for the annual sea turtle nesting events. Witnessing a sea turtle laying her eggs on the beach at night is a truly magical experience.

Both coasts offer a different side of Costa Rica's natural beauty and cultural diversity. Whether you seek thrilling waves and adventure on the Pacific coast or a tranquil, cultural escape on the Caribbean coast, Costa Rica's beaches have something for every traveler.

13.2 Beach Activities

Costa Rica is renowned for its pristine coastlines and stunning beaches, making it an ideal destination for beach lovers and water enthusiasts. Whether you're a sun-worshipper, an adrenaline junkie, or simply seeking relaxation by the sea, the beaches of Costa Rica offer a diverse range of activities for everyone to enjoy. Here are some of the top beach activities to partake in during your Costa Rican adventure:

1. Sunbathing and Relaxation:
   - Lay back on the soft, golden sands and soak in the tropical sun.
   - Enjoy a beachfront massage or yoga session, offered at many coastal resorts.

2. Swimming and Snorkeling:
   - The Pacific and Caribbean coastlines boast calm and crystal-clear waters, perfect for swimming and snorkeling.
   - Explore vibrant coral reefs and swim alongside colorful marine life.

3. Surfing:

- Costa Rica is a world-famous surfing destination with consistent waves for surfers of all skill levels.
- Popular surf spots include Tamarindo, Jaco, and Puerto Viejo, each offering its unique wave experiences.

4. Stand-Up Paddleboarding (SUP):
- Paddle along the coast, enjoying serene views of the shoreline.
- Many beaches offer SUP board rentals and lessons for beginners.

5. Kayaking:
- Explore mangroves, estuaries, and sea caves by kayak, providing a close encounter with the country's rich biodiversity.
- Keep an eye out for howler monkeys, iguanas, and a variety of bird species.

6. Wildlife Watching:
- Costa Rica's beaches are often surrounded by lush rainforests, offering opportunities for wildlife observation.
- Look for sea turtles nesting on Tortuguero Beach or spot sloths in the trees of Manuel Antonio National Park.

7. Beach Volleyball and Soccer:

- Join a pickup game of beach volleyball or soccer with locals and fellow travelers.
- Many public beaches have designated areas for these sports.

8. Horseback Riding:
- Experience the coastline on horseback with guided tours available in various beach towns.
- Witness spectacular sunsets while riding along the shore.

9. Fishing:
- Costa Rica is a premier destination for sportfishing, with opportunities to catch marlin, sailfish, and other big game fish.
- Charter a fishing boat for an exhilarating deep-sea fishing excursion.

10. Bonfires and Nighttime Strolls:
- Enjoy the romantic ambiance of a beachfront bonfire under the starry skies.
- Take moonlit walks along the shore, listening to the gentle waves.

Costa Rica's beaches cater to all types of travelers, from families seeking a relaxed atmosphere to adventure seekers looking for thrilling water sports. The key is to find the beach that aligns with your interests and create unforgettable memories by the sea in this tropical paradise. Whether you're sunbathing, exploring underwater wonders, or riding the waves, the beaches of Costa Rica have something special to offer every visitor.

13.3 Hidden Beach Gems

Costa Rica is renowned for its breathtaking coastlines, and while many of its beaches are popular tourist destinations, there are hidden gems waiting to be discovered by intrepid travelers. These hidden beach treasures offer pristine beauty, tranquility, and a chance to escape the crowds. Here are some of the lesser-known, hidden beach gems in Costa Rica that you won't want to miss:

1. Playa Santa Teresa:
  Tucked away on the Nicoya Peninsula, Playa Santa Teresa is a haven for surfers and nature lovers. The beach is known for its laid-back atmosphere, world-class waves, and lush tropical surroundings. It's the perfect spot to unwind and connect with nature.

2. Playa Montezuma:
  Just a short drive from Santa Teresa, Playa Montezuma offers a unique blend of jungle and beach. The beach is known for its stunning

waterfalls, where you can take a refreshing dip in freshwater pools. This bohemian village is a hidden gem with a vibrant artsy community.

3. Playa Conchal:
   Located in the Guanacaste region, Playa Conchal is known for its unique sand. Instead of typical sand, it features crushed seashells, creating a mesmerizing shoreline. The turquoise waters and coral reefs make it a fantastic spot for snorkeling and diving.

4. Playa Ventanas:
   Nestled on the southern Pacific coast, Playa Ventanas is known for its remarkable sea caves and tunnels. During low tide, you can explore these natural formations and watch the waves crash through the openings, creating a dramatic display of nature's power.

5. Playa Avellanas:
   For those seeking a more secluded escape, Playa Avellanas, also known as "Little Hawaii," offers a tranquil setting surrounded by a lush forest. The beach is famous for its excellent surf breaks and stunning sunsets.

6. Playa Preciosa:

As its name suggests, Playa Preciosa, or "Precious Beach," is a hidden gem on the Osa Peninsula. Accessible by boat, this secluded paradise boasts crystal-clear waters and thriving marine life. It's a great spot for snorkeling and observing dolphins and sea turtles.

7. Playa Uvita:
Located within Marino Ballena National Park, Playa Uvita is known for its iconic "Whale's Tail" sandbar formation during low tide. It's a fantastic place for whale watching, swimming, and enjoying the natural beauty of the Pacific coast.

When exploring these hidden beach gems, remember to practice responsible and sustainable tourism, respecting the environment and local communities. Costa Rica's hidden beaches offer a chance to connect with nature, experience tranquility, and create unforgettable memories away from the beaten path. Whether you're a solo traveler, a family, or a couple, these hidden beach gems have something special to offer.

Chapter 14. Wellness and Relaxation

14.1 Spa and Wellness Retreats

Costa Rica is not only renowned for its stunning natural landscapes and adventure activities, but it's also a perfect destination for those seeking relaxation, rejuvenation, and self-care. Spa and wellness retreats in Costa Rica offer travelers a tranquil escape to balance their minds, bodies, and souls amidst the lush tropical surroundings. These retreats provide a harmonious blend of holistic healing, spa treatments, yoga, and meditation set against the backdrop of pristine rainforests, pristine beaches, and serene mountain getaways.

Key Highlights:

1. Holistic Healing in Natural Settings: Costa Rica's wellness retreats often capitalize on the country's abundant natural beauty. Whether nestled within the rainforest, perched beside a tranquil river, or situated on a remote beach, these retreats embrace nature as a fundamental part of the healing process.

2. Yoga and Meditation: Yoga and meditation enthusiasts will find a haven in Costa Rica. Many retreats offer daily yoga classes in open-air shalas, allowing participants to connect with their inner selves while surrounded by the soothing sounds of the jungle or the gentle waves of the ocean.

3. Therapeutic Spa Treatments: World-class spa facilities at these retreats offer a variety of therapeutic treatments, including massages, body scrubs, facials, and more. Local and exotic ingredients are often used in these treatments, enhancing the overall experience.

4. Healthy Cuisine: Wellness retreats prioritize nutritious and delicious cuisine. Guests can savor organic, farm-to-table meals that cater to various dietary preferences, ensuring a holistic approach to well-being.

5. Detox and Cleanse Programs: Many retreats offer detox and cleanse programs designed to rid the body of toxins and promote holistic health. These programs may include juice fasts, herbal treatments, and personalized wellness plans.

6. Eco-Friendly Practices: Costa Rica is committed to sustainable and eco-friendly practices, and wellness retreats align with this ethos. Many of these retreats implement eco-conscious initiatives to minimize their environmental impact.

Popular Wellness Retreat Destinations:

- Nosara: Known for its yoga and surf culture, Nosara is a tranquil beach town where you'll find numerous wellness retreats.
- Arenal: With its volcanic hot springs and lush rainforests, Arenal offers a serene setting for relaxation and rejuvenation.
- Osa Peninsula: Located in the southern part of Costa Rica, this remote area is perfect for those seeking seclusion and wildlife encounters.
- Guanacaste: The province of Guanacaste is famous for its spa resorts and wellness centers, making it a popular destination for wellness seekers.

Costa Rica's spa and wellness retreats provide an opportunity to disconnect from the fast pace of daily life and reconnect with your inner self. Whether you're seeking a tranquil escape or aiming for a holistic transformation, these retreats offer a range of options to cater to your specific wellness needs. A visit to one of these retreats in the heart of nature can leave you feeling rejuvenated and balanced, making it a memorable part of your Costa Rica journey.

14.2 Yoga and Meditation Centers

Costa Rica, with its lush rainforests, serene beaches, and abundant natural beauty, provides an ideal backdrop for those seeking inner peace and spiritual rejuvenation through yoga and meditation. The country boasts a variety of yoga and meditation centers that cater to practitioners of all levels and interests. These centers not only offer a tranquil environment but also a chance to connect with the local culture and like-minded individuals. Here's a glimpse into what you can expect when exploring these centers:

1. Natural Settings:
   - Many yoga and meditation centers in Costa Rica are set amidst pristine natural surroundings, allowing you to immerse yourself in the sights and

sounds of the rainforest or the soothing waves of the ocean. These settings provide a unique opportunity to connect with nature while deepening your practice.

2. Expert Instructors:
   - Costa Rica's yoga and meditation centers are staffed by experienced and knowledgeable instructors who are passionate about helping you improve your practice. Whether you're a beginner or an advanced practitioner, you can find classes that suit your skill level and objectives.

3. Diverse Offerings:
   - The centers offer a wide range of yoga styles, from Hatha and Vinyasa to Kundalini and Ashtanga, ensuring that you can choose the practice that resonates with you. Additionally, meditation classes, mindfulness workshops, and spiritual retreats are often available for those seeking mental and emotional well-being.

4. Retreat Experiences:
   - Many centers offer retreat packages that combine yoga and meditation with eco-adventures and holistic wellness treatments. These retreats are designed to provide a comprehensive rejuvenating

experience that balances your mind, body, and spirit.

5. Local and International Community:
   - Engaging with fellow practitioners is a significant part of the experience at these centers. You'll have the chance to connect with both local Costa Ricans and fellow international travelers who share your passion for yoga and meditation. This sense of community can be enriching and enduring.

6. Eco-Consciousness:
   - Costa Rica's commitment to sustainability extends to its yoga and meditation centers. Many of them are eco-conscious, practicing responsible and green living, which aligns perfectly with the principles of yoga and meditation.

7. Retreat Locations:
   - While yoga and meditation centers can be found throughout the country, popular locations include the Nicoya Peninsula, the Osa Peninsula, the Arenal region, and the Caribbean coast. Each region offers a unique experience, so you can choose a center that matches your preferences.

Whether you're looking to deepen your practice, seek inner peace, or simply enjoy the tranquility of

Costa Rica, the country's yoga and meditation centers provide the perfect environment to enhance your well-being and connect with the essence of "Pura Vida" – the pure life.

14.3 Hot Springs and Natural Healing

Costa Rica is a land of geological wonders, and one of the most soothing experiences it offers is the indulgence of its natural hot springs. These therapeutic springs are dotted throughout the country, with a particularly high concentration near the Arenal Volcano, known for its geothermal activity.

1. Arenal Hot Springs:
   Nestled at the base of the Arenal Volcano, you'll find numerous hot springs resorts, each offering a unique and relaxing experience. The water in these springs is naturally heated by the volcano's activity, making it rich in minerals and thought to have healing properties. Visitors can soak in a range of pools with varying temperatures, enjoy cascading waterfalls, and even experience mud baths.

2. Tabacon Thermal Resort & Spa:
   Tabacon is one of the most renowned hot spring destinations in the country. It features beautifully landscaped pools that blend seamlessly into the

lush rainforest surroundings. The resort offers a range of spa treatments and therapies, making it a haven for those seeking relaxation and rejuvenation.

3. The Springs Resort & Spa:
   This luxury resort not only provides stunning views of the Arenal Volcano but also boasts a collection of pools with temperatures that vary from cool to pleasantly warm. It's a perfect choice for couples seeking a romantic getaway.

4. Río Perdido:
   If you're looking for a more off-the-beaten-path experience, Río Perdido offers a unique thermal river. This hidden gem is located in a dry tropical forest, and visitors can relax in the soothing river while surrounded by the region's natural beauty.

Natural Healing Properties:
Costa Rica's hot springs aren't just about relaxation; they're also believed to have natural healing properties. The mineral-rich water is said to aid in reducing stress, improving circulation, and soothing aching muscles and joints. Additionally, the hot water is thought to help alleviate skin conditions and even detoxify the body.

Many hot spring resorts also offer spa services, including massages and therapeutic treatments, to enhance the healing experience. It's a holistic approach to wellness, where visitors can soak in the therapeutic waters, immerse themselves in nature, and unwind in a tranquil setting.

Whether you're seeking a romantic escape, a family-friendly adventure, or a personal journey to health and wellness, Costa Rica's hot springs provide an exceptional opportunity to connect with nature while rejuvenating your body and spirit.

Chapter 15. Budget Travel Tips

15.1 Money-Saving Strategies

Costa Rica is a beautiful and vibrant destination, but it can be quite expensive for travelers. However, with some smart planning and a few money-saving strategies, you can enjoy this tropical paradise without breaking the bank. Here are some tips to help you make the most of your Costa Rican adventure while keeping your budget in check:

1. Travel in the Off-Peak Seasons: Costa Rica has a high and low tourist season. If you can be flexible with your travel dates, consider visiting during the low season. This can result in significant savings on accommodations and activities.

2. Choose Budget Accommodations: Costa Rica offers a wide range of accommodation options, from luxury resorts to budget-friendly hostels and guesthouses. By opting for more affordable lodging, you can allocate your funds to other experiences.

3. Self-Catering: Many hostels and vacation rentals have kitchen facilities. Save on dining out by preparing your meals with fresh, local ingredients from markets and supermarkets.

4. Use Public Transportation: Public buses are a cost-effective way to get around Costa Rica. They may take a bit longer than private shuttles, but they are a fraction of the price. Alternatively, consider sharing rides with fellow travelers to split the costs.

5. Embrace Free and Low-Cost Activities: Costa Rica's natural beauty is often the main attraction. Take advantage of the many free or low-cost activities, such as hiking in national parks, swimming in waterfalls, or enjoying the beaches.

6. Buy Souvenirs Wisely: Souvenir shops near popular tourist sites tend to be more expensive. Consider shopping in local markets and negotiating prices for handicrafts and mementos.

7. Use Local Currency: When paying for goods and services, it's often cheaper to use the local currency, Costa Rican colón, rather than relying on credit cards with unfavorable exchange rates.

8. Bargain When Appropriate: In local markets and with independent vendors, bargaining is a common practice. Politely negotiate prices to get the best deals.

9. Explore Lesser-Known Destinations: While popular tourist spots like Manuel Antonio and Arenal are fantastic, lesser-known destinations can be just as beautiful and more budget-friendly. Explore places like Montezuma, Ojochal, or Puerto Viejo for a different experience.

10. Plan and Book in Advance: Booking tours, activities, and accommodations in advance can help you secure lower prices and discounts. Look for package deals or special offers to save even more.

11. Consider Volunteering or Work Exchanges: If you have more time, look into volunteering opportunities or work exchanges in Costa Rica. In exchange for your time and effort, you may receive free accommodation and meals.

By incorporating these money-saving strategies into your Costa Rica adventure, you can enjoy all the natural wonders, cultural experiences, and adventures that this country has to offer while keeping your budget in check. Costa Rica's pura vida lifestyle doesn't have to come at a high cost.

15.2 Free and Low-Cost Activities

Costa Rica is not just a paradise for nature enthusiasts and adventure seekers; it also offers plenty of options for travelers on a budget. While there are high-end experiences available, you can still have an amazing time without breaking the bank. Here are some free and low-cost activities to enjoy in this beautiful country:

1. Beachcombing and Swimming: Costa Rica boasts a coastline of over 800 miles, with many public beaches. Whether you're on the Pacific or Caribbean coast, you can relax, swim, or sunbathe without spending a dime. The warm waters and stunning scenery are always accessible.

2. National Parks and Reserves: While some national parks have an entrance fee, many offer free or low-cost admission. You can explore the rich biodiversity, hike through lush rainforests, and

witness incredible wildlife. Keep an eye out for discounted tickets for students or children.

3. Bird-Watching: Costa Rica is a birdwatcher's paradise, and you don't need expensive equipment to enjoy it. Bring your binoculars and visit one of the many national parks or nature reserves. Keep an eye out for toucans, parrots, and vibrant tropical birds.

4. Hiking and Nature Walks: Many hiking trails are free to access, and they lead to breathtaking viewpoints and hidden waterfalls. National parks like Manuel Antonio and Arenal offer marked trails, or you can explore rural areas and coffee plantations.

5. Yoga and Meditation: Costa Rica is known for its wellness centers and yoga retreats. While some are pricey, others offer affordable classes and workshops for travelers looking to rejuvenate their body and mind.

6. Local Markets: Visit local markets to experience Costa Rican culture and sample authentic cuisine. You can try delicious street food like empanadas or casados (traditional meals) at a fraction of the cost of restaurants.

7. Museums and Cultural Centers: Some museums, like the Gold Museum in San Jose, offer free admission on certain days. Explore the history, art, and culture of Costa Rica without spending a lot.

8. Free Wildlife Viewing: You don't need to book a costly tour to see wildlife. Head to areas like Tortuguero or Corcovado National Park where you can spot turtles, monkeys, and other animals from viewing platforms or along the beach.

9. Volunteer Opportunities: If you have some time to spare, consider volunteering with local conservation projects or community initiatives. This can be a rewarding and low-cost way to give back while immersing yourself in the local culture.

10. Swimming in Waterfalls: Discover hidden waterfalls throughout the country and enjoy a refreshing swim in the crystal-clear pools. Some popular spots include La Fortuna Waterfall and Nauyaca Waterfalls, where the entrance fees are generally reasonable.

Costa Rica offers a wealth of free and budget-friendly activities for travelers. Whether you're a backpacker on a tight budget or just looking to save some money, you can still experience the natural beauty, culture, and adventure that this remarkable country has to offer.

15.3 Bargaining and Negotiating

Costa Rica is a country with a rich and diverse culture, and part of that culture includes the art of bargaining and negotiating. While bargaining is not as prevalent as in some other countries, it is still practiced in various situations. Understanding the dos and don'ts of bargaining and negotiating can enhance your travel experience and help you get the best deals on souvenirs, tours, and local goods. Here's what you need to know:

1. When to Bargain:
   - Local Markets: Bargaining is more common in local markets, especially for handcrafted goods, artwork, and souvenirs.
   - Small Shops: In smaller, family-run shops, you may have more room to negotiate prices.
   - Tours and Activities: Sometimes, tour operators are open to negotiation, particularly if you're booking multiple activities.

2. How to Bargain:

- Be Polite: Always approach bargaining with a friendly and respectful attitude. It's a cultural exchange, not a confrontation.
- Learn Basic Spanish Phrases: Knowing some basic Spanish phrases can go a long way in building rapport with local vendors.
- Comparison Shop: Before bargaining, check prices at a few different places to get an idea of a fair price.
- Start Low: Begin with a price lower than what you're willing to pay and be prepared to meet in the middle.

3. When Not to Bargain:
- Supermarkets and Chain Stores: Bargaining is not customary in larger, established stores.
- Restaurants: Prices in restaurants are typically fixed, so there's no need to negotiate.

4. Negotiating Tips:
- Bundle Purchases: Vendors may offer better deals if you're buying multiple items.
- Cash is King: Cash payments might provide more leverage in negotiating, as some vendors prefer it over credit cards.
- Respect Local Customs: Understand that bargaining may not be suitable in all situations.

Some vendors may not be open to negotiating prices, and it's crucial to respect their decision.

5. Finalizing the Deal:
   - Once both parties agree on a price, it's essential to honor the agreement and complete the transaction.

Remember that the goal of bargaining in Costa Rica is not just about getting the lowest price but also about engaging with the local culture and people. Enjoy the experience, and if a seller isn't willing to meet your price, graciously thank them and move on. Bargaining can be a fun and rewarding aspect of your Costa Rican adventure, allowing you to bring home unique treasures while creating memorable interactions with the locals.

Chapter 16. Safety and Health

16.1 Emergency Contacts

While Costa Rica is a relatively safe destination for travelers, it's essential to be prepared for unforeseen emergencies. Familiarize yourself with the following emergency contacts and information to ensure your safety and peace of mind during your visit to this beautiful country.

1. Emergency Services: In case of any life-threatening situation or immediate danger, dial 911. This will connect you to the local emergency services for police, medical, or fire assistance.

2. Tourist Police: Costa Rica has a dedicated Tourist Police force known for their assistance to travelers. You can reach them at 911 or contact the nearest

Tourist Police station. They are trained to help tourists in multiple languages and can provide guidance and support.

3. U.S. Embassy and Consulate: If you're a U.S. citizen and require assistance related to passport issues, legal matters, or other emergencies, contact the U.S. Embassy in San Jose or the U.S. Consulate in other regions. Their contact information is as follows:
   - U.S. Embassy in San Jose: +506-2519-2000
   - U.S. Consulate in Costa Rica: Contact details may vary by location, so be sure to check the specific contact information for the region you are in.

4. Embassies and Consulates for Other Countries: If you are a citizen of another country, it's advisable to know the location and contact information for your country's embassy or consulate in Costa Rica. They can provide assistance in case of emergencies or lost documents.

5. Medical Emergencies: For medical emergencies, Costa Rica offers a well-established healthcare system. If you require medical assistance, call the local Red Cross (Cruz Roja) at 911. Additionally,

most major cities and tourist areas have private hospitals and clinics with English-speaking staff.

6. Poison Control: In case of poisoning or toxic exposure, contact the Costa Rican Poison Control Center at 800-Poison (800-764-766).

7. Lost or Stolen Credit Cards: If your credit cards or important documents are lost or stolen, contact your bank or credit card company immediately. It's wise to carry a list of emergency contact numbers for your financial institutions separately from your cards.

8. Roadside Assistance: If you encounter vehicle problems while driving in Costa Rica, most rental car companies provide roadside assistance. Keep their contact information handy, and be sure you understand the specific terms and procedures.

9. Consular Assistance: If you face legal issues or need consular assistance, contact your home country's embassy or consulate in Costa Rica. They can provide guidance, arrange legal representation, and help with various consular services.

Remember that while these emergency contacts are essential, it's equally important to exercise caution and practice common-sense safety measures during your stay in Costa Rica. Stay informed about local conditions and be aware of your surroundings to ensure a safe and enjoyable travel experience.

16.2 Health Precautions

Costa Rica is known for its stunning natural beauty and diverse ecosystems, but like any travel destination, it's essential to take health precautions to ensure a safe and enjoyable trip. Here are some important health precautions to keep in mind when visiting Costa Rica:

1. Vaccinations: Before traveling to Costa Rica, it's advisable to consult with your healthcare provider or a travel clinic. Ensure your routine vaccinations, like measles, mumps, rubella, and diphtheria, are up to date. Additionally, consider vaccinations for hepatitis A, hepatitis B, and typhoid, especially if you plan to explore rural areas.

2. Mosquito-Borne Diseases: Costa Rica is home to various mosquito-borne diseases like dengue, Zika, and chikungunya. To protect yourself, use insect repellent, wear long-sleeved clothing, and stay in accommodations with screened windows. Travelers, particularly pregnant women, should be cautious

about the Zika virus, as it can have health implications.

3. Water and Food Safety: While the tap water in many urban areas of Costa Rica is considered safe to drink, it's recommended to stick to bottled water to avoid any potential stomach discomfort. Be cautious about consuming uncooked or undercooked seafood, and ensure that fruits and vegetables are washed and peeled before eating.

4. Sun Protection: The sun in Costa Rica can be quite intense, especially near the equator. Protect yourself from sunburn by wearing sunscreen, a wide-brimmed hat, and sunglasses. Drink plenty of water to stay hydrated, especially in warm and humid climates.

5. Altitude Sickness: If you plan to visit high-altitude areas like Monteverde or Arenal, be aware of altitude sickness. It's a good idea to acclimate gradually and consult a healthcare professional for advice on managing symptoms if necessary.

6. Traveler's Diarrhea: Traveler's diarrhea can be a concern in many parts of the world, including Costa Rica. To minimize the risk, practice good hand

hygiene and avoid street food and uncooked items. Consider bringing over-the-counter medications to alleviate symptoms if needed.

7. Medical Facilities: While Costa Rica has a reasonably good healthcare system, especially in major cities, it's essential to have travel insurance that covers medical emergencies. Know the location of the nearest medical facilities and hospitals in case you need assistance.

8. Prescription Medications: If you're taking prescription medications, ensure you have an adequate supply for your entire trip. Keep your medications in their original packaging, and carry a copy of your prescriptions in case you need a refill or encounter any issues at customs.

9. Insect and Animal Encounters: Be cautious when exploring the lush rainforests and nature reserves. While the majority of encounters with wildlife are safe, it's wise to maintain a respectful distance from animals and avoid feeding them.

By taking these health precautions, you can enjoy the natural wonders of Costa Rica while minimizing potential health risks. Remember that a little preparation and vigilance can go a long way in ensuring a safe and memorable journey in this captivating country.

16.3 Environmental Conservation

Costa Rica is not only celebrated for its stunning natural beauty but also for its commitment to environmental conservation. This Central American gem has earned a reputation as a global leader in sustainability and eco-friendly practices. Travelers to Costa Rica are often inspired by the country's dedication to preserving its pristine landscapes, rich biodiversity, and unique ecosystems.

National Parks and Protected Areas

One of the cornerstones of environmental conservation in Costa Rica is its extensive system of national parks and protected areas. Covering roughly 25% of the country's landmass, these areas are sanctuaries for a wide range of species, including some that are endangered or critically endangered. The protection of these habitats allows travelers to witness the wonders of Costa Rica's wildlife, from the vibrant quetzal bird to the elusive jaguar.

Sustainable Tourism

Costa Rica has embraced sustainable tourism practices, ensuring that the influx of visitors does not harm the environment. Eco-lodges, ecolodges, and environmentally-conscious accommodations are abundant, offering travelers the chance to experience the country's natural beauty without negatively impacting it. These lodgings often employ sustainable methods such as recycling, energy conservation, and local sourcing.

Renewable Energy

Costa Rica stands out as a leader in renewable energy production. The country has a goal to become carbon neutral by harnessing its abundant natural resources. Hydropower, wind, and solar energy are major contributors to the nation's electricity grid. Travelers can witness the eco-friendly initiatives firsthand and appreciate the efforts to reduce the carbon footprint.

Wildlife Protection

The protection of Costa Rica's incredible wildlife is a top priority. Organizations and initiatives work tirelessly to rescue and rehabilitate injured or trafficked animals. Travelers can visit wildlife rescue centers to learn about conservation efforts and even witness some of these creatures up close before their eventual release back into the wild.

Community-Based Conservation

Costa Rica's environmental conservation efforts often go hand-in-hand with community engagement. Local communities are active participants in the preservation of natural resources, and sustainable practices help support their livelihoods. Travelers can interact with these communities, learn about their traditions, and support local eco-friendly initiatives.

Educational Opportunities

For those interested in environmental conservation, Costa Rica provides an exceptional educational experience. Travelers can visit research stations, participate in eco-tours, or attend workshops to gain a deeper understanding of the country's diverse ecosystems and the ongoing efforts to protect them.

Costa Rica's commitment to environmental conservation is an integral part of its identity. Travelers have the unique opportunity to explore this ecological paradise while also contributing to the preservation of its breathtaking landscapes and remarkable biodiversity. Whether you're a nature enthusiast or simply appreciate the beauty of the natural world, a visit to Costa Rica offers an inspiring journey through a land dedicated to safeguarding the planet's ecological heritage.

Chapter 17. Language and Communication

17.1 Spanish Language Basics

When traveling to Costa Rica, having a basic understanding of the Spanish language can greatly enhance your experience. While many Costa Ricans, or "Ticos" as they are affectionately known, speak some level of English, especially in tourist areas, making an effort to communicate in Spanish can open doors to a deeper cultural immersion and more authentic interactions.

Here are some essential Spanish language basics to help you navigate your Costa Rican adventure:

1. Greetings and Politeness:
   - Hola - Hello
   - Buenos días - Good morning

- Buenas tardes - Good afternoon
- Buenas noches - Good evening
- Por favor - Please
- Gracias - Thank you
- De nada - You're welcome

2. Common Phrases:
   - ¿Cómo estás? - How are you?
   - Me llamo... - My name is...
   - No entiendo - I don't understand
   - ¿Dónde está...? - Where is...?
   - ¿Cuánto cuesta? - How much does it cost?
   - Necesito ayuda - I need help
   - ¿Puedes repetir, por favor? - Can you repeat, please?

3. Ordering Food:
   - La carta, por favor - The menu, please
   - Quisiera... - I would like...
   - Una mesa para dos - A table for two
   - El menú del día - The daily special
   - La cuenta, por favor - The bill, please

4. Numbers:
   - Uno - One
   - Dos - Two
   - Tres - Three
   - Cuatro - Four

- Cinco - Five
- Diez - Ten
- Cien - One hundred

5. Direction and Transportation:
   - ¿Cómo llego a...? - How do I get to...?
   - Izquierda - Left
   - Derecha - Right
   - Parada de autobús - Bus stop
   - Baño - Restroom
   - Aeropuerto - Airport

While these basic phrases will help you get by in Costa Rica, remember that pronunciation and regional dialects can vary. Costa Ricans are known for their friendly and patient nature, so don't hesitate to try speaking Spanish, even if your skills are limited. The effort will be appreciated and can lead to memorable encounters with the warm and welcoming people of this beautiful country.

17.2 Communication Tips

When traveling in Costa Rica, effective communication can significantly enhance your experience and interactions with the local culture. While Spanish is the official language of Costa Rica, and many Costa Ricans speak at least some English, here are some communication tips to help you navigate your way through this beautiful country:

1. Learn Basic Spanish Phrases:
   While you don't need to be fluent in Spanish, learning some basic phrases can be incredibly helpful. Phrases like "Hola" (hello), "Gracias" (thank you), and "Por favor" (please) will go a long way in demonstrating your respect for the local culture.

2. Use Polite and Friendly Language:
   Costa Ricans are known for their warmth and friendliness. Using polite language and addressing people with "Señor" (Mr.) and "Señora" (Mrs.) or "Don" and "Doña" followed by their last name is appreciated.

3. Non-Verbal Communication:
   Non-verbal communication is essential in Costa Rican culture. A friendly smile and maintaining eye contact can convey a lot. Ticos (Costa Ricans) appreciate a warm and approachable demeanor.

4. Pronunciation Matters:
   Pay attention to your pronunciation, as it can affect how well you are understood. Practice the

correct pronunciation of place names and common phrases to minimize confusion.

5. Use Hand Gestures Sparingly:
   While hand gestures can be helpful, they can also vary in meaning between cultures. It's best to use them sparingly and to rely more on verbal communication.

6. English in Tourist Areas:
   In popular tourist destinations, you'll find that many people, especially those working in the tourism industry, speak English. However, it's still appreciated when visitors make an effort to speak some Spanish.

7. Pointing and Gesturing:
   When in doubt, pointing at what you want or need can be quite effective. Whether it's a menu item or a location on a map, a simple gesture can help bridge language barriers.

8. Be Patient:
   If you encounter language barriers, don't get frustrated. Costa Ricans are patient and understanding, and they will appreciate your effort to communicate.

9. Ask for Help:

If you're unsure about something, don't hesitate to ask for help or clarification. Ticos are known for their helpfulness and are generally happy to assist.

10. Use Technology:

Having a translation app or a phrasebook on your smartphone can be a valuable resource when you need to translate or look up specific words or phrases.

By following these communication tips, you'll be better equipped to connect with the friendly people of Costa Rica and immerse yourself in the rich culture and natural beauty that this Central American gem has to offer.

17.3 Local Phrases and Slang

When visiting Costa Rica, understanding a few local phrases and slang words can enhance your travel experience and help you connect with the friendly Ticos (Costa Ricans). While Spanish is the official language, Costa Rica has its own unique expressions and idioms that reflect the country's culture and way of life. Here are some essential local phrases and slang to familiarize yourself with:

1. Pura Vida: This is perhaps the most famous Costa Rican phrase. It means "pure life" and is used to convey a positive outlook, expressing happiness and contentment. Ticos often use it as a greeting or to describe a great experience.

2. Tico/Tica: These terms refer to Costa Rican men (Tico) and women (Tica). It's common to hear locals use these nicknames to describe themselves or others.

3. Mae: This word is equivalent to "dude" or "buddy." You'll hear it frequently in casual conversations.

4. Gallo Pinto: This is a traditional Costa Rican dish of rice and beans mixed together, often served as part of breakfast. Locals might refer to it simply as "Gallo."

5. Chorreada: If you're a fan of Costa Rican street food, you'll want to try a chorreada, which is a type of corn pancake. They are delicious and a popular snack.

6. Tuanis: This slang word means "cool" or "awesome." If something impresses you, you can say it's "tuanis."

7. Jama: When you're hungry, you'll ask for "jama." It's the local way of saying "food" or "a meal."

8. Chunche: The word "chunche" is a catch-all term for an object, thing, or gadget. It's often used when someone can't remember the name of something specific.

9. Maje: This term can be somewhat similar to "fool" or "idiot." Use it carefully, as it can be considered impolite if used inappropriately.

10. Tico Time: In Costa Rica, time is often more flexible, and schedules can be relaxed. "Tico time" refers to this more laid-back approach to punctuality.

11. Limonense: This word refers to someone from the city of Limón on the Caribbean coast of Costa Rica. People from Limón have their own unique accent and dialect.

Learning these local phrases and slang words can help you communicate with locals and immerse yourself in the rich culture of Costa Rica. Don't be afraid to use them during your travels; Costa Ricans are known for their welcoming and friendly nature and will appreciate your effort to embrace their language and expressions.

Made in the USA
Monee, IL
07 January 2024

51350095R00109